HOT
STUFF

A Brief History of Disco

John-Manuel Andriote

HarperEntertainment
An Imprint of HarperCollinsPublishers

HarperCollins books may be purchased for educational, business, or sales promotional use. For information please write: Special Markets Department, HarperCollins Publishers Inc., 10 East 53rd Street, New York, NY 10022.

FIRST EDITION

Designed by Amy Halperin

Library of Congress Cataloging-in-Publicaton Data
Andriote, John-Manuel.
  Hot stuff : a brief history of disco / by John-Manuel Andriote.
    p. cm.
  ISBN 0-380-80907-9
    1. Disco music—History and criticism.   I. Title.

ML3526 .A53 2000
781.64—dc21   00-044968

01 02 03 04 05 RRD 10 9 8 7 6 5 4 3 2 1

TO THE MUSIC-MAKERS WHO GIVE US
GOOD TIMES DURING THE HARD TIMES

CONTENTS

ACKNOWLEDGMENTS

First I want to thank Hamilton "Boogie Shoes" Cain for suggesting I write a book about disco. Hamilton was my original editor on this book, and his enthusiasm for my work and this project have been inspirational. His special favor of critiquing the first draft, a gesture of friendship and confidence in the project, is much appreciated.

Others at HarperCollins also have worked hard to give birth to this book. I'm grateful for the fresh, frank critique of the first draft by Tia Maggini, my interim editor. Tom Dupree, my third and ultimate editor, was enthusiastic about the book from the beginning. Thanks for that, Tom, and for explaining how Chubby Checker got his name. Special thanks to Yung Kim for her excitement about the book, resourcefulness, good humor, and availability. It has been a pleasure to work with you, Yung.

Thank you to John Hawkins for agenting the book and becoming a friend. Thanks also to Warren Frazier for his role in all those high-powered contract negotiations.

Thank you to those who took time to be interviewed for the book, helping to educate me about the finer points of disco music and culture. Thanks to the musicians, record companies, and photographers who let me use their photos. Particular thanks to Bobby Miller for making available photos from his "photographic diary of Studio 54"—*Fabulous!*—and especially for the terrific picture of Donna Summer.

Thank you to the friends who have shared with me exuberant nights of dancing. What an irrational, ecstatic, erotic, silly, FUN thing dancing is—it's been great to enjoy it with you.

As always I have been blessed with wonderful people who encouraged me through this project—and even enjoyed the disco stories I've served up from my research. In particular, thanks to Scott Foster and Kenny Hill for their willingness to listen and tweak as needed. Thanks once again to my professor and friend Delvin L. Covey for following my progress on *Hot Stuff* in our letters and offering steady support for its (and my) progress. Thanks to other friends for their kindness and indulgence, particularly Ron Caringi, Laura Goldstein, Rod Mercer, Victor Omelcenko, and Christopher Zukowski.

My abiding gratitude to my family, the people who knew me in the seventies and still share the good and bad times with me in the twenty-first century. Thank you to my mother, Anna Andriote, for always listening, encouraging, and loving me. The friendship I've found with my "little" sister Sue has gladdened my heart and helped me go forward. Thank you, Sue. And thanks to my sister Pam for participating in the making of memories during our teen years in the seventies when we joined other kids in our neighborhood in such innocent mischief as streaking and sneaking swigs of Boone's Farm. Though he isn't here to read this, I am deeply grateful to my late father, Manny Andriote, for passing on to me his great love of music, particularly black music. I didn't know back when Dad was playing those Wilson Pickett and Junior Walker albums in the sixties, I'd grow up to realize—as in so many other areas of life—he was so right.

Thanks to each and all of you. May you enjoy many happy days, magical nights, and an eternity dancing with angels.

ix • ACKNOWLEDGMENTS

INTRODUCTION

When the Hues Corporation sang "Don't tip the boat over" in their 1974 number-one hit "Rock the Boat," they could have been speaking for a nation rocked by the disorienting upheavals of the sixties, the outraged grief of Vietnam, and the deflowering scandal of Watergate. Americans wanted to escape the stresses and strains of the day, and tens of millions of them in the late 1970s found the outlet they needed in the music and club scene of the disco era that "Rock the Boat" helped usher in.

The line between fantasy and reality blurred in the discos, and the music and lights transported revelers to another plane where they could be stars shining in the Me Decade constellation. For some, the recreational drugs that were so abundant on the club scene provided an accelerated mode of transportation. For everyone, getting *down* was the only thing that mattered on a Saturday night.

Disco started with a trickle and then flooded the clubs and airwaves. It began as a crossover phenomenon in itself—black and Latin music played in mostly white gay clubs. Disco began its crossover to the white, heterosexual middle class because cool straight people often frequented gay clubs where the music was played. One of the unique social forces of disco, in fact, was its ability to bring together gay and straight, black and white, like no other popular music before it. People of all colors and orientations united in the name of Fun.

Like any social force, this one gathered steam by word of mouth as clubgoers and deejays talked up their favorite dance tunes and clubs. Disco records sold like hotcakes because people bought them after hearing them in the clubs—even if they weren't hearing the songs on the radio at first. By the time the recording industry and radio clued in that something major was going on, and began marketing directly through the clubs, disco music was already popular enough to monopolize the airwaves.

Emerging from black American rhythm and blues, soul, and funk, "disco" music started as a kind of producer's music, made by unknown studio musicians. The members of the disco group Chic ("Dance, Dance, Dance," 1978) were refused admission to Studio 54 because no one recognized them, even though a couple of their songs were then burning up the clubs. But the genre soon produced a galaxy of its own stars, including Gloria Gaynor, Thelma Houston, Grace Jones, and biggest of them all, Donna Summer.

The music was so wildly popular in the late seventies that, as early as 1976, it was rare that a non-disco record made it to the number-one spot on the major trade charts. Several times that year alone as many as six of the Top 10 records were disco-flavored. "Mainstream" recording artists from a variety of musical backgrounds—including Ethel Merman, Dolly Parton, and

Frank Sinatra—cashed in on the phenomenon, spinning out disco records that turned to gold as though by musical alchemy.

Feeding into and off the cult of celebrity beginning to take hold of the country in the late seventies, Studio 54 opened in April 1977, almost instantly becoming the center of the disco world—a "Disneyland for adults," as one regular described it. Fantasy for those on the inside, Studio was a nightmare for the many more kept at bay outside the club's fabled velvet ropes because they didn't have the right look for the night's "tossed salad" of a crowd inside. There were other "celebrity" discos like Studio 54 that drew the pretty and rich and those who wished they were. But by the end of the seventies, there were an estimated twenty thousand discotheques throughout the U.S. Two hundred disco-format radio stations and television shows from *Soul Train* to *Sesame Street* also contributed mightily to the cultural phenomenon by which disco music and culture saturated the American mainstream.

Disco music literally brought America to its feet in every manner of discotheque imaginable—kiddie discos, roller discos, even discos for the elderly. For every up-and-comer dying for a glimpse of Andy, Liza, and Truman at Studio 54, thousands of ordinary folk escaped the grind of their workaday lives by loosening up and losing themselves in the joyous sensuality of disco. Soul and salsa and a whole lot of gay camp colored the music. Spinning the new twelve-inch "disco discs," deejays also spun the webs that gathered up and dispersed everyone's cares, making the 125-beats-per-minute of disco music seem like the heartbeat of life itself.

In 1978, disco's hottest year, disco queen Donna Summer hit number one with "Hot Stuff" and "Bad Girls." Her anthem

"Last Dance," from that year's disco movie *Thank God It's Friday,* was the number-one disco hit for the year. The Bee Gees were "Stayin' Alive." After its release in December 1977, *Saturday Night Fever* made disco "safe" for the white, middle-class mainstream. With the Bee Gees putting a white face on what was essentially black music, it was suddenly okay to admit publicly that one liked disco. What grist for the wheels of popular culture it became! From fashion to television shows to Hollywood movies, the culture of the disco was commercialized almost beyond recognition.

By 1979, a backlash was already building. Deejay Stephen Dahl—described by *Newsweek* as "a militant anti-disco agitator"—organized a "Disco Demolition" in Chicago's Comiskey Park. Dahl invited everyone who shared his distastes and prejudices to burn disco records in a large bonfire. Hundreds joined him who shared the sentiment "Disco Sucks," a saying which had become an increasingly popular way of distancing onself from the garish, self-indulgent spectacle that disco had become. For many, though, the rise of anti-disco sentiment let them mask their prejudices toward blacks and gays in the guise of "musical taste."

Throughout the eighties and nineties, disco-style music, in all its unapologetic glory, continued to be wildly popular in the gay clubs where it had first found a welcome. Many other nightspots programmed their music from one or a combination of several post-disco generations of what is now simply called "dance music." From house music to dance-pop, from rap to techno, every dance-music style since disco shows evidence of its ancestry.

Two decades after the "Disco Demolition," disco is the Hot New-Old Thing. In the winter of 2000, Cher's "neo-disco" album

Believe earned the sixties siren a Grammy Award for best dance recording after achieving triple platinum sales within months after its debut the year before. In the summer of 1999, Donna Summer released a new live recording of her biggest hits. Cyndi Lauper remade "Disco Inferno." The previous year, Whit Stillman's film *The Last Days of Disco* had tracked a group of young wanna-bes—precisely the kind who would have remained beyond the velvet ropes of the actual club—smiling their way inside a Studio 54–like disco in Manhattan. Mark Christopher's own 1998 film *54* looked at the legendary club through the eyes of a young working-class guy who becomes a bartender there. That same year, *Saturday Night Fever* opened as a stage show in London, eventually moving to Broadway in the fall of 1999.

Almost everywhere you looked at the start of the new millennium, twentysomethings were running around in seventies clothes. Oldsters over thirty and youngsters under twenty alike were crowding into dance clubs for "retro" nights to hear disco music. The twenty-year nostalgia cycle has come back around. In the seventies, the fifties were revived in movies and TV shows. Now it was the seventies' turn. Disco music certainly ranked at the top of any list of the positive legacies of that particular decade. In 2000, those old disco tunes were still as danceable as they had been two decades earlier. Dozens of Web sites on the Internet are devoted to disco, connecting enthusiasts to others like themselves throughout the world. Disco is still tremendously popular throughout the world among gay and straight and every hue of the human rainbow, and vast quantities of disco-style music are sold each year.

It seems safe to say that after two decades of "just say no"— to drugs, unsafe sex, cigarettes, and cholesterol—a lot of restless people are ready for the "good times" that disco helped to create and celebrate. It's clear that millions of people throughout the world still agree that the music whose only purpose was to get your spirits up and to help you get down is the *only* music for dancing.

1

HOW IT BEGAN

It's cold tonight and there's a line waiting to get into what everyone's calling the "hot new disco" here in my nowhere-in-particular hometown. As we approach the door, the thumping beat vibrates the walls. I can hear Donna Summer's "Last Dance" as clearly as if I were standing on the dance floor. Red and blue lights flash through the steam-covered glass of the door. Here I go! Five bucks? I guess I've got to get over the sticker shock of this disco scene. I guess it's the price you pay for the experience.

Would you look at that dance floor? There are lights in the floor itself! Multicolored fog is rising from the floor, dry ice and hot lights fusing to create a kind of indoor bog pulsing with very human life. Men and women become strangely gesturing shadows through the atomized veil. You can't see the girls' stiletto heels or the guys' platform shoes. The fog smells like chocolate. It makes my daiquiri taste a little funny. Maybe a rum and coke wouldn't be as bad with a little chocolate edge?

Lights twirl overhead, ricocheting off the big mirror ball spinning above the middle of the dance floor, reflecting off the mirrored walls.

The deejay is on a Donna Summer riff. He just went from "Hot Stuff" right into "MacArthur Park"—without a pause. Come to think of it, "Last Dance" lasted a long time. It must have been one of those new twelve-inch disco discs. They've been around in the big-city clubs for a while, but we're a little slow out here in God's country catching on to those city things.

That's probably why disco didn't catch on here until after *Saturday Night Fever* came to town last winter. People wanted to get out a bit, catch a movie, after all those long, slow winter nights. The Blizzard of '78 really made us all a little restless. Ever since that movie, kids are going out to the disco. At first they were embarrassed to be seen here. Everybody thought disco was just for gay guys or black folks. John Travolta showed them that straight white guys can like disco—and even be good dancers. Now some of them are embarrassed to run into their own parents, and their parents' friends, here! The younger kids go to the roller rink on Saturday mornings for their kiddie disco party.

Mostly everyone comes here. This place has been around since the sixties, when it was called The Dial Tone. It's no Studio 54. It's out on this back road in the sticks. You don't have to be famous or gorgeous to get in. But you do have to be cool. And the joint sure gets jumping! Sometimes my friends take a puff or toot of things those kids who used to be called the bad kids at school bring along to do out in the parking lot. When that disco beat—and whatever they puffed or tooted—kicks in, they're sliding out on the dance floor with everyone else, just like those slide drums in the music.

It's great to be here. What a week I've had. What a life I've had—at the ripe old age of twenty. I guess like everybody else in America in 1978, I just want to relax and cut loose a little bit. All right, now, there's that Alicia Bridges song. I love the nightlife, too! What a scene! Disco rules!

Rule it did—at least for a little while. The rat-a-tat-tat of the disco beat that brought us to our feet in the seventies seemed to swell out of the depths of our souls as it transported us somewhere ethereal and, some even said, divine. It lifted us up and out of ourselves, helping to heal the wounds that the sixties and the first part of the seventies had inflicted on the nation's bruised psyche.

Like other dance music before it, disco appeared when it did because it was what people needed. In troubled times, people seek the kind of release that comes from intense physical activity like athletics and sex. Disco blended athletics and sex in one joyous belt of exuberance that shook—and shook up— the land with its mixture of hedonism and hilarity. In the late seventies, at disco's peak, getting down with the music was the best way to get your mood up and get on with your life. That was a major challenge for a lot of people at the time.

For all their liberation movements and monumental achievements, the sixties were a dark night of the soul for many Americans. Free love and flower power ran smack up against a level of hatred and violence that stood out even in such a hate-filled and violent century. From assassinations of beloved leaders to the British Invasion of rock musicians, from the war in Vietnam to the war at home for civil rights, from walking on the moon to flying higher than the moon at Woodstock, the sixties was a decade of sharp contrasts and social upheavals.

The decade's idealism and strife carried into the seventies.

Even the most upstanding citizens found their faith in America challenged by the harsh economics and politics of the new decade. "The years that followed the sixties were like the proverbial 'morning after,'" write Peter Jennings and Todd Brewster in *The Century*, their sweeping overview of the twentieth century. "The cupboards were bare, the once-mighty passion for public acts now spent, along with much of America's heretofore indefatigably optimistic spirit."

The seventies began with more violence when four student antiwar protesters were killed by National Guardsmen at Ohio's Kent State University on May 4, 1970. High unemployment and what was called "stagflation" went hand-in-hand with oil shortages and a dawning awareness of the environmental impact of the nation's optimistic expansion after World War II. Only a year after celebrating America's withdrawal from Vietnam in 1973, Americans' faith in their government was shaken to the core with the Watergate scandal and disgraced resignation of President Nixon. As Jennings and Brewster so aptly put it, the seventies started with "the feeling that American civilization had entered into an irreversible decline."

Many Americans withdrew from the powerlessness they felt in the bigger world into their own little worlds, where they could at least feel they had a modicum of control. Tom Wolfe proclaimed the seventies "the Me Decade" because of this self-absorption. Books with titles like *Looking Out for Number One* proliferated. Hang-ups were out, "self-actualization" and hedonism were in. Guilt, limits, and restraint were passé. The day you were living in may have been the first day of the rest of your life, but it was the only one that mattered. If tomorrow was too painful to think about, there were numerous pills, powders, and other pharmaceuticals to promote a happier frame of mind. Many availed themselves of this kind of help in the seventies.

Drugs weren't the only thing that could transport you to more joyous realms of consciousness. There was dance music to soothe the soul, stir the feet, and shake the booty. As early as 1972, disco music was taking shape in "underground" places—gay clubs, black and Latino clubs, and clubs in blue-collar neighborhoods where white kids cut loose on Saturday nights. There is widespread disagreement as to when "disco" became a distinctive style of music. Some say the 1973 chart-topping hit "Love's Theme," by the Love Unlimited Orchestra, was the first identifiable disco hit. Others say it was Gloria Gaynor's 1975 hit "Never Can Say Goodbye" that made the singer "the first disco diva." Most everyone agrees that Van McCoy and the Soul City Symphony's "The Hustle," in 1975, made it clear that something new and exciting was happening.

If it's hard to pinpoint which song was the first disco song, that's because disco was a fusion of several genres of music—mainly rhythm and blues, soul, and funk. It didn't happen all at once, but rather it evolved. Early disco music was distinguished by the way it drew together various types of music into a distinctively lush blend—with an insistent beat. It was frequently likened to the big-band sound of the thirties because of its lively rhythm, brassy horns, and textured sound.

Disco music and dancing may have seemed like merely the newest variation on an old theme, but the fusion of the music and the social frisson it created were almost entirely new. Together, the music and the culture it spawned produced some of the most enduring images of the seventies. In such a decade, that says a lot for how exciting disco was at the time and how well it served the deep human urge that inspired its creation: the urge to dance.

DANCE, DANCE, DANCE

The need to escape in the ecstasy of music, the need to dance, was hardly new to the seventies. Rhythm has always been as central to human life as the beating of our hearts. Dance, the oldest of human arts, is the body's natural response to rhythm. Even cave people danced and made rituals of their dance as they worshiped or entreated their gods.

In the years since cave people shook and swayed, dance in the Western world—and the music accompanying it—has also evolved. Early folk dances that still survive, such as the Irish jig and the Italian tarantella, were embellished and formalized in the Renaissance, when the royal courts created the minuet while peasants danced the lively gavotte. In the late eighteenth century, dancing became an activity for couples who moved gracefully to the three-quarter time of the waltz.

In the early 1900s, Irving Berlin's "Alexander's Ragtime Band" got people doing the Turkey Trot to the "ragged time" music. In 1912, a kind of dance fever set in as couples slinked across ballroom floors to the Latin rhythms of the tango—the first of several "Latin invasions" of the twentieth century. But it wasn't until after World War I that dance and dance music took a turn that would shake it up and shimmy it down the ladder of years to become disco in the 1970s.

Jazz music, deeply rooted in African-American rhythms, its four-four beat nicknamed "ragtime," brought 1920s flappers to their feet to do the foxtrot and quick step. As *New York Times* music critic Stephen Holden described the Roaring Twenties beat, "Buoyant and high-stepping, it was a rhythm propelled by a hysterical urge to throw off the chains of the past, live for the moment and if possible become airborne." Jazz Age partiers expressed the rhythm of the times in such lively dances as the Charleston, the Suzy Q, the shimmy, the black bottom, and the shag. During the Great Depression, desperate men and women entered dance marathons hoping to win the monetary prizes that would help them support their families. In one marathon, participants danced for 3,780 hours—more than twenty-two weeks—for a prize of one thousand dollars, about twenty-six cents an hour.

Ragtime was joined in the late thirties by a musical immigrant to America, Latin music. In the years after the tango had titillated America, South American rhythms found their way into other American dances such as the foxtrot and Charleston. The Brazilian samba spiced up ballroom dancing after its introduction to the U.S. at the 1939 World's Fair. The conga, mambo, and merengue added their own dash to the mix.

In the late thirties and into the forties, American dance music took yet another turn with the smooth but lively sound of swing. Big bands led by Glenn Miller, Guy Lombardo, Tommy Dorsey and Jimmy Dorsey, Harry James, Benny Goodman, and others drew big crowds wherever they traveled.

But World War II put a damper on dance music as so many men went off to war and left their sweethearts at home to swoon alone to lovelorn ballads on the radio. While GIs started the racy and gymnastic jitterbug at USOs, anxious hearts back in the U.S.A. were calmed by crooners like Frank Sinatra and Bing Crosby and by the lush sounds of Ella Fitzgerald and Perry Como.

Kicking up the feet would come in the fifties. Early in the

decade, the Latin-inspired cha-cha reflected the nation's post-war optimism and prosperity as Americans saw their lives reflected back at them in the new medium of television. Large groups jumped and kicked to the bunny hop. But the fifties would long be remembered for giving the world something that literally revolutionized both music and dance: rock and roll. When Elvis Presley—soon to be dubbed the King of Rock and Roll—appeared on *The Ed Sullivan Show,* millions of viewers saw only the top half of his body: His provocative hip gyrations were considered too much for family viewing. Soon, however, millions of viewers could hear the newest rock songs and see teenagers doing the latest dances on the weekly TV show *American Bandstand.*

New dance styles had been scandalizing the uptight since time immemorial. In the early 1800s the waltz shocked them because partners had to embrace to do it. Boston Mayor John "Honey Fitz" Fitzgerald, grandfather of President John F. Kennedy, banned the turkey trot in that puritan capital. The Reverend Billy Sunday in 1915 denounced the tango as "the most hellish institution that ever wriggled from the depths of perdition." In the 1920s the United Dancing Masters of America condemned the Charleston as "too vulgar to deserve official recognition." No sooner had the Big Apple, a dance in the 1930s, emerged from a black nightclub in Columbia, South Carolina, than the prudes blasted it for combining "all the worst elements of the Charleston, the Black Bottom, Trucking, Shag—and the Virginia Reel!" Even the Lindy, or jitterbug, was suspect because it was "preferred by groups whose main objective is the enjoyment of expressional orgies."

Rock and roll gave the world a new style of singing, and created the need for new, faster dances. None of them matched the twist. The twist introduced a new idea in popular dance: a solo dance, done in place, as simple as toweling off, and appealing to all ages. The song that launched the twist craze, simply titled "The Twist," was first recorded in 1959 by Hank Ballard and the Midnighters. But it was a nineteen-year-old chicken plucker named Ernest Evans whose recording of the song a year later sent dancers twisting across dance floors everywhere. Evans was known as Chubby Checker—a nickname given him by Bobbie Clark, wife of *American Bandstand* host Dick Clark, as a playful variation on the name of another popular singer, Fats Domino.

One dance floor in particular was associated so strongly with the twist that it gave rise to its own version of the song that inspired it. For years, the Peppermint Lounge was a Times Square watering hole for the down-and-out. But about the time Chubby Checker's song climbed the pop-music charts, New York's fun-loving upper crust "discovered" the Peppermint Lounge. Overnight, the lounge became the hottest club in New York. Celebrities such as Greta Garbo, Noël Coward, and Tennessee Williams made it their nightspot of choice. Meanwhile, the lounge's original customers sat gunning their motorcycles at the curb, puzzled by the sudden interest in their old hangout. The club's own house band, Joey Dee and the Starlighters, recorded "The Peppermint Twist," further linking the now-famous club with the dance craze that had swept the nation.

The twist established new ground rules for dancing: anything goes. And you didn't necessarily need a partner to go there. A slew of new dances followed the twist in the sixties. Touching was out, individuality was in. With names like the Watusi and the funky Broadway, the dances of the sixties, like so many popular dances before them, revealed their African-

American roots. Others, like the pony, the frug, the mashed potato, the monkey, the hitchhiker, the swim, the shake, and the skate, grew out of discotheques around the country and were practiced regularly in the basement rec rooms where American teenagers danced and dreamed their way through the growing pains of adolescence.

Nothing was like the twist, though. The Top 100 songs of 1962 included no less than seven twist songs. That year Chubby Checker's second version of "The Twist" reached number one. As pop culture observer Albert Goldman put it, "With the twist, America learned how to 'get down.' "

LE DISCO

Americans had been dancing to recorded music for years by the time the twist came along. In 1899, the owner of the Palais Royal Saloon in San Francisco installed an Edison phonograph with four listening tubes, activated by a nickel deposited in a slot. It wouldn't be until repeal of Prohibition in January 1933, though, that the jukebox became a fixture of bars, taverns, and restaurants. "Juking" was a word derived from the Gullah dialect of African-Americans in the sea islands of Georgia and South Carolina. It meant "disorderly" or "wicked." It was in pursuit of a bit of more or less orderly wickedness, companionship, and escape that people gravitated to their neighborhood "juke joints"—usually a bar with a jukebox—during the Depression years.

The concept of public spaces devoted to dancing developed further with the arrival of rock and roll. But it was already being explored by the French during World War II. Joining the French words *disque* (record) and *bibliotheque* (library), the discotheques (literally "record libraries") of wartime Paris served cocktails along with their patrons' favorite jazz records. Dancing to "American"-style music was considered decadent by France's German occupiers. Even this early in its history, the disco was a place where restless and rebellious spirits could find freedom.

The most famous early discotheque in Paris was Paul Pacine's first Whiskey à Go-Go, which opened in 1947. *Le jazz hot* and Scotch whiskey made for an intoxicating brew inside the Whiskey, whose walls were covered with tartans and the lids of whiskey cases. Within a decade every major city and resort in Europe had its own version of the nightclub. Meanwhile, another discotheque in Paris, Chez Castel, had become the discotheque of choice for the local avant-garde, and strictly off-limits to tourists and strangers.

In 1960, Régine Zylberberg, the daughter of Polish-Jewish immigrants, opened Chez Régine after starting out a decade earlier as a ladies'-room attendant at Whiskey à Go-Go. For a month Régine kept curious would-be patrons at bay outside the Parisian nightspot, posting a DISCO FULL sign each night and hosting a private party inside for her friends. One night shortly after Chez Régine finally opened to the public, the American cast of *West Side Story* came into the club carrying the twist records they had brought from New York. *"Qu'est-ce que c'est?"* asked Régine. The twist, they told her. Overnight, Chez Régine became the French answer to the Peppermint Lounge.

In New York, another Frenchman, Oliver Coquelin, opened Le Club on New Year's Eve 1960. The Upper East Side discotheque offered everything you would expect of a joint whose moniker was what Albert Goldman called "that snobbish little monosyllable." A sense of exclusivity and a setting conducive to sensory pleasures drew the crowds to Le Club. An initiation fee ($150) and annual dues ($35) kept away the hoi polloi and foreshadowed the snootiness of the "celebrity" discos to come in the seventies.

Also paving the way for the 1970s discos were the 1960s rock discos. In the wake of the British Invasion, another (Americanized) Whisky-A-Go-Go opened on January 11, 1964—this one in Los Angeles. *Entertainment Weekly* described it as "one part discotheque, one part rock-star launching pad, one part hip hangout." Go-go girls spun records and frugged in glass cages while more than two thousand people "made the scene" each night. A number of rock artists even found their big break at the Whisky, including Otis Redding, the Byrds, the Who, Jimi Hendrix, Black Sabbath, and the Doors, who were discovered there in 1966.

Back in New York, a club called Arthur opened in May 1965. Sybil Burton, the first former wife of the actor Richard Burton, was Arthur's proprietress. In marked contrast to Le Club, La Sybil wanted to create "a playground for all the bright little shopgirls, hairdressers, and fledgling models who were just then emerging as a new urban class," as Albert Goldman put it. Fun was more valuable to Burton than self-important attitudes. Like the Peppermint Lounge, though, the heat and light that Arthur generated drew the rich and famous, too. Opening night found newly defected ballet superstar Rudolf Nureyev, dressed in a brown Beatles suit, twisting the night away with Sybil herself.

Former Peppermint Lounge regular Terry Noel, known for his creative dancing, was brought into Arthur on its second night to serve as deejay. If he could generate half the excitement in spinning discs that he generated on the dance floor, went the reasoning, he (and the club) would be a success. Playing a mix of rock and soul, Noel hit bingo. Not only did he become the first deejay to "mix" records, but the colored lights he set blinking in time with the music set the style for the next decade, when lights and music would be mixed in head-tripping ways never dreamed before.

Radcliffe Joe, *Billboard* magazine's disco editor in the seventies, noted, "Lighting is to disco as love is to marriage, as tonic is to gin, as music is to dancing. Disco would not be disco without it." The first commercial light show in the U.S. was at San Francisco's legendary Fillmore West. But it was once again in New York that all the elements of what would become disco—lights, dance music, and the underground counterculture—came together. The Electric Circus, located in an old Polish workingman's club on St. Mark's Place on the Lower East Side, opened in 1967. During its brief three-year run, it was advertised as "The Ultimate Legal Entertainment Experience. Air-Conditioned in more ways than one. Come. (Stoned.)" The terms "mind-blowing" and "freak show" were among the colorful descriptions of the club.

By the time the Electric Circus closed in 1970, the discotheque concept was seen as tarnished at best. The youthful voices of protest against the Vietnam War and the free love of the sixties flower children were both quieting down as hippies grew up and into the mainstream establishment. Rebellion was cooling, and for many rock music itself wasn't as cool as it once had been. Some of the biggest rock groups—among them the Beatles; Blood, Sweat & Tears; Led Zeppelin; and the Who—disbanded, changed members, or moved on to other ventures.

The jet set, who had brought style and even respectability

to the discotheque world, were moving on in search of night-time pleasures away from what had become the low-life world of leftover hippies, thugs, and other ne'er-do-wells. The clubs dwindled to a handful, and they were generally not places that the monied and with-it would want to be seen. "It was time," said *Billboard*'s Radcliffe Joe, "for disco to move underground, lick its many festering wounds, and map its directions for the future."

UNDERGROUND

"Underground" in those days meant unpublished addresses, elevators up several flights of an old building, and word of mouth. It was in the underground that society's "outcasts"—blacks, Hispanics, gay men, the working class—found community and flourished. Small dance floors in vacant buildings, even private homes, became havens from an intolerant world, where patrons could enjoy profound freedom and the purest of democracies. All were equal in the Land of Pleasure. From this ethnic, sexual, and socioeconomic mélange would arise the extraordinary musical, social, and cultural phenomenon that became disco.

One of the earliest magazine articles describing the "sudden" popularity of disco failed to note that the music and club scenes were already well established, if undetected as yet by the mainstream, at the time of the article's 1976 publication. *Newsweek* said, "The group most responsible for keeping discos alive was the homosexual community." Sound engineer Alex Rosner told the magazine, "The pioneering done in the disco field has been done by gays, with the blacks and Puerto Ricans following." He added, "The common denominator there is oppression."

For many gay men in the early seventies, New York was the center and capital of the world. It was the setting for a massive "coming-out" party as gay people tested their newly liberated identities a couple of years after the 1969 riots at the Stonewall Inn. But it was still a place where the "real" lives of gay men were hidden by the night from prying heterosexual eyes. Some of these men found the sense of acceptance they craved with their brothers in the shirtless, sweaty tribes they became when they danced together. Through the informal social networks that linked gay people in the years before AIDS brought them together, these men knew they could find kindred spirits at the small underground discos like the Sanctuary, the Loft, and the Tenth Floor.

The Sanctuary, originally a disco called the Church intended for straight celebrities, was located in an old German Baptist church in the Hell's Kitchen section of Manhattan. While Albert Goldman described it as "the most decadent discotheque in history" because of its diabolic decor (in keeping with its location), others saw it differently. In a 1998 *Village Voice* article called "The Last Days of Gay Disco," Peter Braunstein noted, "The Sanctuary epitomized the post-Stonewall era, when gay men had won the right to dance intimately without worrying about the police." From his booth at the Sanctuary's altar, Braunstein said the deejay "administered a thumping sacrament to legions of adoring parishioners, who celebrated his mastery of slip-cuing by showering him with quaaludes while dancing the original, gay version of the bump."

The Loft was literally deejay David Mancuso's loft apartment on Broadway just north of Bleecker Street. It didn't get going until after 3 A.M. on a Sunday, when the liquor-selling discotheques closed for the night. Free membership, a low three-dollar cover charge, free punch, cookies, coat check, and a super mix of music made it a terrific club. Regulars remember it as an exceptional club because of the sexual and racial mix of the people who danced together there. Women, blacks, Latinos, straight and gay men—they all mingled at the Loft.

Novelist Andrew Holleran found this kind of democracy at the Tenth Floor when he started going there in 1971. The Tenth Floor was situated in two smallish rooms in an old building on West Thirty-third Street. The club drew the good-looking men who frequented the gay resorts on Fire Island, a beautiful strip of beach and dune off the Atlantic side of Long Island popular among gay people for many years. The Tenth Floor's opening in 1971 provided these men with a place to continue the revelry that began that summer with the opening of the Ice Palace in Fire Island's Cherry Grove. The late journalist Nathan Fain recalled the Ice Palace as "the laboratory and proving ground for madder music, stronger drugs, and wholly abandoned styles of undress and undulation." In his 1978 novel *Dancer from the Dance,* Holleran described the intermingling of sorts and types in a fictionalized "Twelfth Floor." He wrote, "It was a democracy such as the world—with its rewards and penalties, its competition, its snobbery—never permits, but which flourished in this little room on the twelfth floor of a factory building on West Thirty-third Street, because its central principle was the most anarchic of all: erotic love."

Of course erotic love has great appeal to heterosexuals, too, so there would frequently be straight women and their comfortably straight male friends somewhere in the crowd. Despite the mix, the fact was that the early gay discos were among the few places where the gay men who frequented them felt safe and able simply "to be." The clubs ran the risk that letting in too many straight people would keep gay men away. And without the masculine sexual energy generated by these men the discos typically spiraled into a voyeuristic spectacle. As Holleran described the "ending" of *Dancer*'s Twelfth Floor, "The second year it was too famous, and too many people wished to go. Film stars and rock stars, and photographers, and rich Parisians, and women from Dallas came to look, and it was finished."

Looking back at those earliest days of what became known as disco, Holleran says, "It was still an underground world, like Alice in Wonderland: You've gone through this doorway and inside was this incredible world you didn't know existed. That's what the discos were like." But then something happened and it became harder to find the sexually charged, hidden places where the music that habitués called "dark disco"—the deepest of rhythm and blues with the most driving beat, played at the penultimate moment before collapse at the end of a long night—could be heard. What was often referred to as "the gay sound," as well as the exclusivity of the disco scene, was giving way to something else entirely.

The bigger uptown discos, with their mixing of music, races, genders, and sexual orientations, would provide the real bridge for disco music and energy to "cross over" into the so-called mainstream. Le Jardin, an essentially gay club, occupied two floors—the penthouse and basement—of the seedy Diplomat Hotel on West Forty-third Street. In contrast to Le Jardin's stylishness, Flamingo offered what Anthony Haden-Guest in *The Last Party* understatedly called an "inventive cabaret" atmosphere. Mock crucifixions and live pigs feasting on magazines tossed into their pen were among the club's more outrageous amusements. It also popularized the kinds of theme parties—black parties and white parties, for example—that would prove such a draw for other discos in the coming years.

But it was Infinity, opened by nightclub impresario Maurice Brahms in the fall of 1975, that successfully melded uptown chic and downtown edge—the magical mix so essential to the success of a discotheque. Although Infinity drew a gay crowd when it opened, the club soon attracted the party crowd, the heterosexual social set who could make or break a club with their support or lack of it. As with other clubs, as soon as Infinity made a name for itself, what was called "the scurve" arrived: young, single, middle-class straight men and women trying to get picked up. Beginning two years later, Infinity's energy and appeal, as well as its deterioration, would be repeated when two of the club's regulars, Steve Rubell and Ian Schrager, opened Studio 54, the most famous disco of them all.

DISCO DOWN

In the meantime, something was happening to the music of the night: disco was beginning to take shape as a distinctive style of dance music. In 1973, what came to be called simply "disco" was just emerging. Disco's roots in black and Latin music, and its association with gay men, would give the music its uniquely exuberant emotional and sexual energy. But those roots and associations also caused mainstream Americans—the white middle class—to resist disco at first. They had always resisted what the recording industry called "race music" until someone gave it a white face and thereby declared it "safe" for red-blooded Americans—that is, straight, white men.

While rock and roll morphed into its various offshoots in the late sixties, it was rhythm and blues (R & B) soul, and funk music that were really taking off in popularity. Of course, Detroit's homegrown black-owned record label Motown had been producing successful black singers and big hits for years. No party in the sixties was complete without the danceable tunes of the Supremes, the Four Tops, Marvin Gaye, Smokey Robinson and the Miracles, or, after they came on the scene in 1968, the Jackson 5. Motown excelled at "crossover" music, getting white folks to loosen up and dance to the tunes that were already moving the feet and stirring the soul of black America.

R & B, the beating heart of disco, dates back to the period during and just after World War II. After moving to northern cities for higher-paying jobs, black Americans from the South wanted a newer style of music. The result was the urban sound of rhythm and blues. R & B grew out of what was called jump blues, a late 1940s style of uptempo, jazzy blues. Jump blues usually featured a vocalist in front of a large horn-driven orchestra or midsized combo. The style is distinguished by a driving rhythm, intensely shouted vocals, and honking tenor sax solos. The lyrics are nearly always upbeat, even swaggering. Jump blues bridged the older, small band blues and the big band jazz sound of the 1940s. Among the most popular vocal artists of this style were Dinah Washington, Betty Carter, and Sister Rosetta Tharpe, a gospel-music star who also indulged in secular music.

African-American gospel artists brought a powerful emotional exuberance to their music. Song lyrics took on physical life as the gospel singer "spoke" with his or her whole body. The music's often lively percussive rhythms and the bone-deep cry for freedom and justice at the heart of its words stirs both the souls and bodies of worshipers. As music historians point out, black music is deeply connected to what is going on with black people. It isn't coincidental that in the 1930s and 1940s black artists created new styles of upbeat, cheerful music during one of the nation's most economically depressed times. People needed a lift, and foot-stomping, holy-rolling music was an excellent way to get it.

Despite their use of the same styles of music, the black Pentecostal churches that nurtured gospel artists in the 1940s considered jazz and blues—even though they were made by black artists—to be "hell's own music." Gospel artists like Sister Rosetta Tharpe, however, brought those very styles into the Pentecostal church, the most ecstatically emotional of denominations. The Reverend James Cleveland, gospel's biggest-name singer for three decades, also leaned toward rock and roll and other pop sounds. These musicians, like other black musicians after them, provided bridges between musical eras—spanning two styles of music, innovators in each one—as faster dance music evolved over the latter half of the twentieth century.

Elvis Presley, the King of Rock and Roll himself, sometimes attended an integrated black church in Memphis where gospel music was the featured fare. He is certain to have felt the physical power of music there, and definitely expressed his music in physical terms. R & B itself provided one of the most important foundations of rock and roll with its emphasis on rhythm and shouted vocals. Although it kept the quick tempo and intensity of jump blues, R & B featured sparer instrumentation and emphasized the song rather than improvisation. Essentially it was blues chord changes with a pronounced backbeat. Artists such as Ray Charles, Ruth Brown, the Drifters, the Coasters,

Fats Domino, and Sam Cooke were among the leading names of American rhythm and blues in the 1950s.

In the 1960s, R & B was urbanized and commercialized into soul. Different cities produced their own versions of soul. In New York, Philadelphia, and Chicago, the music involved vocal interplay and smooth productions. Curtis Mayfield was the ultimate Chicago soul singer and songwriter. Detroit's Motown created a pop-oriented sound that blended gospel, R & B, and rock and roll, putting smooth vocals over a typically heavy, even beat that essentially updated the doo-wop style of the 1950s. In the South, the music was harder-edged, relying on those jump blues–style rhythms, raw vocals, and honking horns. Among the most famous soul singers of the sixties were Wilson Pickett, Junior Walker, and of course the still-reigning Queen of Soul, Aretha Franklin.

In the late sixties, soul singers James Brown and Sly Stone introduced yet another new sound in R & B: funk. Funk put the rhythm out in front of a song's melody and harmony, giving it a more authentically African texture. Brown's funk was stripped down, while Stone's was wilder and drew more from rock and roll. George Clinton's band Parliament was a well-known funk group whose sound was described as "disco-dance rhythm . . . with a funk bottom." Eddie Kendricks's 1973 "Keep On Truckin' " also provided a bridge between the sound of funk and the distinct arrangements of disco. Other "bridge" artists whose early 1970s music could be considered either funk or disco include Earth, Wind & Fire ("Shining Star"), Kool & the Gang ("Jungle Boogie"), Carl Douglas ("Kung Fu Fighting"), and the Ohio Players ("Fire").

One distinctive style of R & B arising out of black America

in the early 1970s was named after another city. That was the smooth, sophisticated urban sound of Philadelphia International Records. "T.S.O.P. (The Sound of Philadelphia)" is the best example of what was called "the Philadelphia sound." Recorded in 1974 by Philadelphia International Records' twenty-eight-member house band, Mother, Father, Sister, Brother (better known as M.F.S.B.), the album that included the single *Love Is the Message*, went gold that year. The single became the theme for *Soul Train,* television's black version of *American Bandstand.* It was one of the earliest identifiable disco songs. Unlike the music produced by other black-oriented labels, which continued to focus on soul in the early seventies, the Philly Sound was unique. Its lush orchestration and lively beat made for some of the most textured—and dance-inspiring—popular music ever made. Groups like the O'Jays, the Three Degrees, and Harold Melvin and the Blue Notes brought gold to Philadelphia and joy to dancers everywhere.

Although the early disco-music scene was dominated by Motown and Philadelphia International in 1974–1975, other early and influential styles of disco originated in New York and Miami. The New York sound was strongly influenced by Latin dance music. It featured heavy orchestration that combined the fast dance rhythms of salsa with syncopated drumming and lots of strings. Salsa, the Spanish word for "sauce," was a hot and spicy style of music rooted in the African-tinged rhythms of the Caribbean, particularly Cuba. In the 1920s, Cuban and Puerto Rican immigrants arrived in New York's Spanish Harlem, bringing their instruments and musical styles. Afro-Caribbean rhythms meshed with American jazz in the 1940s to become Latin jazz, creating the first mambo craze in the U.S. In the early 1970s, Fania Records, a New York company known as the "Latin Motown," was the first to promote Puerto Rican music infused with other cultural elements as salsa.

The Miami sound featured sassy horns, Caribbean percussion, and rhythm guitars—think K.C. and the Sunshine Band. Formed in 1973, the band had a big international club hit with their debut single, "Blow Your Whistle." They found fame with "That's the Way (I Like It)," which reached number one in 1975. But it was one of the backup singers on "Blow Your Whistle" who would hit it big with another song penned by Harry Wayne "K.C." Casey and his collaborator Rick Finch—and propel disco music further toward its eventual peak. George McCrae, who sang with his wife, Gwen McCrae, was catapulted from unknown to chart-topper when he recorded "Rock Your Baby" in 1974 and was later credited with having helped launch the disco "movement."

In 1975, another unknown, a former cosmetician from Newark, New Jersey, named Gloria Gaynor, released the first extended-play song recorded especially for the discos, the hit "Never Can Say Goodbye." That year, New York deejays proclaimed Gaynor the first "queen of the discos." Besides furthering the popularity of the best-known dance of the disco years, Van McCoy and the Soul City Symphony's "The Hustle" won a Grammy in 1975 for best performance by an orchestra. It's easy to forget that early disco music got its unique sound by bringing a dance beat out in front of the strains of traditional orchestral instruments, particularly stringed ones.

By 1975, another force was building—this one in Germany—that would soon unite with American R & B and take disco music to new heights. "Euro-disco" not only put the bass line of a song out in front, it also added electronic sounds unknown before in American music. *Newsweek* described

Euro-disco as "an impressionistic, almost symphonic mix of electronic rhythms and spacey synthesized sound concocted by producer Giorgio Moroder." The Munich producer started with a German group called Kraftwerk (German for "power plant"), whose first hit in 1975, "Autobahn," was a twenty-two-minute concatenation of mechanical rhythms, electronic beeps, and monotone vocals.

Moroder explained how Euro-disco changed the sound of dance music—and upped its energy level. "The disco songs we had before 1975 had drums," he said. "Just normal drums, like a rock group. Then in 1975 we started to put in the bass drum. We called it 'four on the floor.' One, two, three, four! We kind of exaggerated." He added, "You watched people dancing and as soon as the song came out with that kind of heavy bass, people liked it."

In the U.S., Silver Convention pioneered Euro-disco by combining electronics with orchestrals in its number-one 1975 hit "Fly, Robin, Fly." But the sound's real first lady was Moroder's personal discovery, Donna Summer. Her hit that year, "Love to Love You Baby," drove dancers to frenzied peaks of pleasure with its electronic cracking whip and Summer's simulated orgasms. Albert Goldman said, "More than any recording in recent years, 'Love to Love You Baby' restored to pop music its highest goal: the inducement of ecstasy." The album of the same name was the first of Summer's gold albums.

Already it was becoming clear that something was happening in the public's musical tastes. More artists were drawn to disco as a distinct style. Vicki Sue Robinson turned the beat around in 1976. Thelma Houston begged, "Don't Leave Me This Way." Heatwave was raising the temperature with "Boogie

Nights." Soon disco became the hot new music that could breathe new life into the long-established careers of singers from other areas of pop music. Even rockers were cashing in on the growing popularity of disco music. The most notable example was the Bee Gees. After years of cranking out Beatles-like tunes, the Bee Gees finally hit the top again in 1975 with "Jive Talkin'."

The head of one disco-oriented record label said Americans "are seeking escapism . . . a respite, however fleetingly, from the seemingly insurmountable hassles of gasoline lines, high food bills, uncertainty about whether they will have enough heating oil to keep warm during the winter, and the growing dilemma of trying to find and keep a roof over their heads." Commenting on the music and the mood it inspired, Vince Alletti, a vice president in the disco division of Warner Bros. Records, said, "Disco is positive, it's about love and good feelings; it even gets a little snappy sometimes, but it's a very positive energy. At its best, it's ecstatic."

Hot as it was among those who danced in the discotheques, disco in the bicentennial year was still mainly a big-city phenomenon. Investors were reluctant to lay out money for discotheques because they thought disco would be just another short-lived fad. Major record labels were skittish about the long-term survival of disco. To keep their audiences dancing, deejays had to search record shops for new and exciting dance music, much of it imported from Europe and Latin America. As Fred Gershon, a lawyer and partner of entertainment mogul Robert Stigwood of RSO (the Robert Stigwood Organization), put it, "Disco was happening. But it was not yet the worldwide craze it became. It was the very smart set and the gay set. Which was sometimes the same set. It hadn't spilled over."

Before radio, television, and Hollywood caught on to disco, the music found other ways to reach its public—mainly through the discotheques, thanks to the deejays. In the disco world, there were no bigger stars than the club disc jockeys. *Newsweek* called them "gurus of the night." They were travel guides of sorts, as well. John Geraldo, a deejay at San Francisco's discotheque the Stud, said, "An experienced deejay will take you on a trip." Spinning and mixing tunes, the deejays could take you up, down, and turn you around before you knew what hit you. Jim Burgess, a top disco deejay in New York, said, "The real trick is to get people dancing to the next record before they even realize they're doing it."

The "gurus of the night" had to have an instinct for what would get the people dancing. Without this insight, there would be empty dance floors, and eventually empty clubs. To be a fine spinner of songs, deejays needed a finely balanced combination of charisma and expertise. They had to be able to gauge the mood of an audience and spin tunes that would guarantee energy and excitement for a night of festive partying. Early in the disco years, they had to do it with what today would be regarded as primitive sound equipment and seven-inch 45s and LPs that didn't lend themselves to easy mixing.

Unlike dance music today, with its made-for-deejays introductions, breaks, and consistent beats per minute, early disco music and the equipment used to play it—in those pre-CD years—challenged deejays to be innovative in their efforts to get people up and boogieing. Jimmy Yu, who began his fifteen-year career as a spinner in Miami in 1974 before returning home to New York in 1977, said, "I would always mentally put myself on the dance floor before every mix." Yu recalled the "prehistoric days" when almost all his mixes had to be "chop mixes." He explained, "Only if two songs had almost identical BPMs [beats per minute] could you blend them together, and even then, by the end of the night I had one raw finger on each hand from long-term dragging on a turntable that wouldn't give in."

With improvements in sound equipment, Yu said the deejay's job got a little easier. "Once pitch controls became available I was able to become more creative in my mixing," he said. "Searching and finding distinct similarities in orchestration, breaks, or vocals between two songs, thinking two or three mixes ahead of what was on and being able to read and control a crowd creatively all became fun yet challenging."

Another innovation of the disco years also made the deejay's job easier, this one by New York disco deejay Tom Moulton. In 1975 Moulton got the idea for extending dance records from the standard seven-inch vinyl format to twelve-inch discs. The longer format allowed record jocks to spin the sides, creatively remix the songs, and, most important, sustain the mood set by a particular song. Mood was everything in the discos. So of course a special "disco disc" was needed. The higher fidelity of the new extended-play format offered something close to the sound of the original twenty-four tracks of the studio tape recorders.

The twelve-inch dance single was the record industry's first new commercial format in nearly thirty years, and it would become one of disco's lasting legacies. As with most innovations in disco music, it was a small record label that first capitalized on Moulton's innovation. Salsoul Records—a small, Latin-music-oriented company until disco put it at the center of the international popular-music scene—was the first to release a twelve-inch 45 rpm single, Double Exposure's "Ten Percent." The format was mainly intended for deejays, but soon enough the disco-loving public wanted their own long-play versions of their favorite dance tunes. The first twelve-inch single available for the general public was Tavares's 1976 crossover hit "Heaven Must Be Missing an Angel."

Another challenge to deejays in the early days of disco was finding enough records to keep their mixes fresh and exciting. Since the concept of record spinning had first caught on in the 1950s—think of the record "hop"—club deejays had to provide their own record library. That could be a very expensive proposition for pioneering disco deejays in the 1970s, who at the time earned between twenty-five and thirty dollars a night, working only the few nights a week that the clubs were open. But if a club deejay wanted to work, he had to keep an up-to-date collection of records. Because of their ability to promote new music, radio disc jockeys and record retailers were the beneficiaries of free promotional albums from record companies. But early on, club spinners weren't considered industry insiders and had to fend for themselves.

The major record labels at the time saw disco as a passing fad, focusing on the popular and lucrative pop/rock format. But something was happening at the musical grassroots level, and the music industry would eventually wake up to it when it caught the inspiring scent of money to be made. That something was the popularity of dance music played in the discos, as dancers and their friends bought up the records they were hearing there. Even before they were played on the radio, popular disco tunes could sell as many as half a million copies in the twelve-inch format, one side featuring an extended vocal version of the song and the flip side an instrumental version of the same tune.

The record labels releasing the music that the deejays were playing noticed this phenomenon. And it was phenomenal because traditionally record sales were boosted by radio airplay. Early in the disco years, though, the music wasn't being played on the radio. So when a hit like George McCrae's "Rock Your Baby" reached the top of the pop-music charts merely from exposure in the clubs, the big record labels were interested. They finally looked at deejays as legitimate and important players in the disco business. Now the labels' view was that, as Robert Summer, president of RCA Records, put it, "The importance of the club deejays can't be overestimated. They monitor the tastes of the audience."

The record companies realized that with hundreds, even thousands, of new discotheques sprouting up around the country, there would be a greater demand for exciting dance records. RCA Records was at the front of the pack at the time with the Hues Corporation's 1974 megahit "Rock the Boat." Right about then, a small Miami-based label called TK Records released George McCrae's "Rock Your Baby." Midland (later Midsong) Records followed quickly with Carol Douglas's "Doctor's Orders." These million-sellers proved to the record companies that disco was both viable and profitable.

No one needed to convince Neil Bogart, owner of Casablanca Records, of disco's profitability. The label of Donna Summer, the Village People, the Ritchie Family, Meco, Paul Jabara, Lipps, Inc., and a host of other well-known disco artists was instrumental in disco's emergence from the underground into the mainstream. Bogart was particularly interested in Euro-disco, and became a committed fan and producer of it after Donna Summer's "Love to Love You Baby" earned her international fame and gave Casablanca a major crossover hit.

Billboard underscored the emerging popularity of disco and the central role of the club deejay by creating a disco-news department and disco-record chart compiled by Tom Moulton. The chart relied upon input from designated deejays across the country. The record companies began adding the names of individual deejays to their lists of recipients of promotional records, which were either mailed to them or delivered by a record label's promoters. But as disco spread beyond New York, San Francisco, Los Angeles, Boston, and Miami—its earliest centers—and clubs seemed to be opening everywhere, it became harder to provide product to individual deejays. Record companies were deluged with requests for promotional records to the point that they realized they needed a new way to distribute their music.

The mutually beneficial solution came from the deejays themselves. In the summer of 1975, New York spinners David Mancuso (whose Manhattan apartment became the Loft disco on weekends), Eddie Rivera, and Steve D'Aquisto formed the New York Record Pool to serve as a clearinghouse for promotional records. The pool gathered all the new releases from the record companies and distributed the records stamped "For Disco DJs Only" to its member deejays. By getting out the promotional pressings weeks before their public release to the pools in New York and those that were formed in other cities, the deejays could build interest in a new record before it hit the stores. By early 1979, record companies were sending out as many as three thousand promotional records per release.

Among the initial fifty members of the New York pool were the city's most popular deejays, including Tom Moulton (who went on to head his own record label, Tom 'n' Jerry Records) and David Todd (who later headed RCA's disco division). Given the demigod status these deejays enjoyed in the disco world, it shouldn't be surprising to note that there were clashes among them almost from the time the first pool was organized. Co-founder Eddie Rivera left the New York pool only five months after its founding, describing it as an undisciplined group of ego trippers. Rivera drew away a good number of the city's ethnic spinners and formed the considerably larger International Disco Record Center (IDRC). The problems in the New York pool were typical of the record pools formed throughout the country as internecine battles erupted among highly individualistic deejays.

Disco music had several other hurdles to scale before finally bursting out of the clubs, onto the airwaves, and into the culture—and they were high ones. As *Billboard*'s Radcliffe Joe noted, certain economic problems were at that point keeping disco bottled up. He pointed out that the "stylized, formulated, synthesized, faceless form" of the music had made it almost impossible to translate its dance-floor appeal to commercial sales. Radio was reluctant to give the format its full support, particularly with no big-name disco artists. This meant limited exposure for disco music. But an even more insidious problem also held disco back. It was what Joe described as "the still taboo sounds of black and Hispanic music" compounded by the embrace and involvement in the music by gay men. As Joe concluded, "Gay support of and creative input into the disco sound now meant that it was no longer just ethnic [black and Hispanic], but gay as well."

Smart gamblers would not have bet on disco's acceptance by the mainstream at this point. Something was needed that would give a new spark to disco and finally push it up and over the top. What would it be?

NIGHT FEVER

In 1977, what Albert Goldman described as a "two-stage explosion" provided the answer. The first was Studio 54, the second the movie *Saturday Night Fever*. The nightclub would show that the new, grand concept of the discotheque as a pleasure palace could work. And the movie would reveal to many beyond the core of the early disco scene that disco music and dance offered release and a good time to everyone.

In a June 1976 cover story in *New York* magazine called "Tribal Rites of the New Saturday Night," journalist Nik Cohn explored his theory that a new generation of young, mainly working-class people who had avoided the rock-induced angst and drug-induced psychedelia of the sixties were responsibly going about their workaday lives during the week—and then "exploding" at the discos on Saturday night. Cohn believed the roots of the newest generation of Saturday night revelers reached back to the fifties, "the golden age of Saturday nights."

At the center of Cohn's story was "Vincent," an eighteen-year-old Italian who was devoted to his mother and sold paint in a hardware store all week. Although Cohn later acknowledged that Vincent was really a composite of several characters (and that he'd made up much of the article), the young dreamer would become bigger than life for many. Vincent was the best dancer and king of 2001 Odyssey, the disco in the Bay Ridge area of Brooklyn that Cohn described in the article. "Third-generation Brooklyn Italian, five-foot-nine in platform shoes," wrote Cohn, Vincent "owned fourteen floral shirts, five suits, eight pairs of shoes, three overcoats, and had appeared on *American Bandstand.*" Everybody knew him, and when he accepted their tributes he was as "gracious as a medieval seigneur." Asked what was his greatest aspiration, Vincent said, "I want to be a star . . . someone like a hero."

A year and a half after the publication of "Tribal Rites," twenty-year-old Tony Manero would become a hero to millions as the Vincent-like character in *Saturday Night Fever.* Cohn's article had caught the attention of two key people, both of them financially interested in seeing disco finally take off—RSO's Robert Stigwood and his film development director, Kevin McCormick. Stigwood had already released two successful musical films, *Jesus Christ Superstar* and *Tommy.* And, as it happened, the Bee Gees recorded for RSO Records and the group had already (and successfully) tested the waters of disco music. Add a few Hollywood-style tweaks by *Serpico* screenwriter Norman Wexler; cast in the lead the sexy twenty-three-year-old John Travolta, who had already gained attention in a touring company of *Grease,* on Broadway, and in the TV sitcom *Welcome Back, Kotter;* set it against the hard realities of 1970s American life—and the outcome was a fantastically successful movie.

Saturday Night Fever became one of the top-grossing movies of 1977, with revenues at upwards of $200 million. The soundtrack, a double LP released in late 1977, became the biggest-selling soundtrack album ever, selling more than thirty-two million copies worldwide. No fewer than ten of its cuts were hit singles in either the U.S. or the U.K. Six reached number one, including the Bee Gees' "Stayin' Alive," "How Deep Is Your Love," "Night Fever," and "If I Can't Have You," sung by Yvonne Elliman, who had portrayed Mary Magdalene in *Jesus Christ Superstar.* Radcliffe Joe said the movie "created an avalanche of demand for the sounds of disco in places where, just short weeks before, disco dared not tread."

How did it do that? How did *Saturday Night Fever* become, as Joe saw it, the generation- and era-defining movie, the *Hair* for the seventies? How could one movie become what Joe called "the catalyst that propelled the concept to center stage of American entertainment enterprises"? It did it by appealing to a wide cross-section of the moviegoing public, in particular to conservative Middle America. *Saturday Night Fever* transmuted the black, Hispanic, and gay associations of disco into something safe for white heterosexual Americans. By giving disco the faces of John Travolta and the Bee Gees, disco became okay to enjoy, permission granted. As Elvis Presley had done for rock and roll, the Bee Gees put a white face on what was essentially black music. They even sang in the falsetto style popular among black groups in the seventies. Almost overnight, there was no need to apologize anymore for tapping your foot to the snappy rhythm of disco music.

Just as Manhattan enticed and intimidated Tony Manero and his dead-end friends in Brooklyn with its allure of glamour and adventure, the heart of New York City also pulsed with an alluring rhythm that echoed across the East River to the borough of Queens. It was there that Steve Rubell and Ian Schrager opened one of their earliest discos, called the Enchanted Garden. A converted golf-course clubhouse, the disco looked good and was popular with kids from Brooklyn, Queens, and Long Island—despite the fifteen-dollar cover charge. But the Enchanted Garden still fell short of its owners' ambitions. As Robert Caravaggi, a regular, put it, "You could see Manhattan in the distance, maybe fifteen miles away. And you could see that that was where Steve Rubell wanted to go."

Go there he did. On Tuesday night, April 26, 1977, Rubell and his business partner Schrager opened Studio 54 in a building that had started life fifty years earlier as the home of the San Carlo Opera Company before becoming a radio and television soundstage for CBS. No one predicted the frenzy of interest the club would generate among those wanting to get in, and among the paparazzi eager to photograph the lucky ones who were literally handpicked to get in. Carmen D'Alessio, a Peruvian "P.R. sorceress," as *Vanity Fair* called her, contributed her hosting talents and her list of eight thousand color-coded names of the rich and famous. The colors designated different categories of customers: "wealthy, young, gay, powerful, sedate." D'Alessio boasted, "I know everybody. The beautiful, the rich, they are all my friends."

Many of the five thousand she invited to the opening-night party showed up. Cher was there, as were Margaux Hemingway, Brooke Shields, and other major and minor celebrities. Others couldn't get in, including Warren Beatty, Kate Jackson (a star of the popular seventies TV show *Charlie's Angels*), and Henry Winkler, "the Fonz" on TV's *Happy Days*. Describing the disco's opening night in *Esquire*, New York journalist Henry Post said, "That night New Yorkers experienced their first disco theater, a mammoth space with lights and sets that rose and fell from the ceiling creating a spectacular and overwhelming environment unlike any other." A large crescent-shaped man in the moon snorting from an oversized coke spoon—"the Moon and the Spoon," as it was fondly known—was a particular crowd pleaser. Darting through the revelers were the young waiters clad in black tights, satin trunks, and tank tops who bore pricey $2.50 cocktails and, often, Rubell's "party favors" for special guests from his own amply stocked pharmacopoeia.

When applications for membership went out, eighteen thousand people eagerly sought to pay the $150 per person annual cost (before it opened, seventy-five dollar memberships were offered to the "right people"), and save three dollars off the ten-dollar cover charge. But membership didn't guarantee admission on a particular night if an individual didn't strike the doorman as offering the "right" qualities (celebrity status, beauty, and outlandish getups helped). Steve Rubell talked about "tossing a salad" and "painting a picture" to describe the seemingly arbitrary yet quite intentional way in which the club's doormen—Anthony Haden-Guest called them "lords of the door"—decided who would get inside and who would be left to gawk and grouse outside. The exclusivity that made Studio 54 such a hot spot would later contribute to the club's undoing as the hip and trendy got fed up with the abusive treatment they frequently received outside Studio 54's velvet rope.

But as long as the party inside was hot, it was very hot indeed. Not long after its opening, *Time*'s "discoguide" described Studio 54 in a way that made it clear that disco, and the idea of the discotheque, had come of age. Every element of disco's history—the select crowd, the music, the lights, the idea of the discotheque as a festive refuge—came together in "fast, loud, and frenzied" Studio 54.

When *Saturday Night Fever* premiered on December 16, 1977, a group of Studio 54 regulars—a list that had almost immediately included Liza Minnelli, Truman Capote, and Andy Warhol, as well as other "celebs," as they came to be known—

started with a dinner at Tavern on the Green. From there it was on to the disco for yet another party for Bianca Jagger with yet another white horse. During the Blizzard of '78 in early February, Studio 54 was packed. Some diehards actually skied to the club. Devotion to pleasure—and certainly addiction to the substances frequently used to enhance it—was a powerful drive.

That cold and snowy winter, the beginning of what would become disco's hottest year, it seemed nothing, least of all inclement weather, could keep discomaniacs from their appointed rounds. Thousands of nightspots throughout the country pumped out the disco sound. Millions of discogoers grooved on the tunes, dressed to the nines in test-tube fibers and feeling as if they were the brightest stars in the night sky. With the commercial explosion of disco, radio finally woke up to the phenomenon. Now disco could be heard anytime, anywhere.

2

WHERE IT WENT

New Year's Eve 1977. Five thousand tickets, about twice the club's legal occupancy, have been sold for what Studio 54's owners promise will be the "most spectacular evening ever." Tickets are a hefty forty dollars. "Think of the money, the money!" Studio's resident hostess Carmen D'Alessio gushes to her friends. The gold metallic invitations feature a striking photo of striking-looking Grace Jones, the entertainment for the night of nights.

The winter air is charged with the excitement starting to spread across the country since *Saturday Night Fever* opened in December. The movie seems to be touching something in the American psyche. The Bee Gees' "How Deep Is Your Love," from the movie soundtrack, is number one on *Billboard*'s Hot 100 chart. Other disco hits are climbing the pop charts, including Andy Gibb's "(Love Is) Thicker Than Water," Chic's "Dance, Dance, Dance (Yowsah, Yowsah, Yowsah)" Santa Esmeralda's "Don't Let Me Be Misunderstood," and Odyssey's "Native New

Yorker." On the disco charts, Donna's Summer's "Once Upon a Time" is running neck and neck with Cerrone's "Supernature" as the most popular club hit in the country.

In less than a year, Studio 54 has become the most famous disco in the world, the gathering place of the "haute société de disco," as *Esquire* put it. Photos of disco-loving movie stars, European royalty, and throngs of wacky-looking characters are featured each week in four-year-old *People* magazine. In a growing culture devoted to celebrities, only the news that New York City's "Son of Sam" mass murderer David Berkowitz is shopping for a publisher for an authorized biography can hope to compete with gossip about what the famous are doing at Studio 54 at 2 A.M. on a weeknight.

Despite the hype for the party to beat all parties, and the praise heaped on it afterward, things at Studio 54 didn't go quite the way they were planned. In fact, they gradually spiraled out of control until the enchanted evening became a night from hell for many of the New Year's revelers. Here's how someone who was there described the scene that night: "It was a frightening night," said Henry Post, recounting that fateful New Year's Eve in an *Esquire* article. "Many ticket holders couldn't get inside Studio 54. Those who did were pushed, shoved, and stepped on in the overcrowded space." Grace Jones was never paid for her performance, noted Post, nor did she receive the costumes that Ian Schrager told her she could keep. To top it off, he said, "Grace Jones's microphones gave out completely in the middle of the last song, after faltering all evening." He added, "The most spectacular evening ever was an artistic embarrassment. Grace Jones was in tears after the show, knowing that her audience would assume it was her voice and not the microphone at fault."

Studio 54's New Year's Eve bash might have turned into a crush of disasters, but that didn't prevent *Discothekin'* magazine from naming it number-one disco in the country for 1977. In the cold winter of 1977–78, disco was hot and Studio 54 was the hottest spot in the world.

Hearts racing and hopes rising as they primped for a Saturday night out at the disco, tens of millions of Americans in 1978 almost overnight had caught an acute case of boogie fever. Whether working at a car wash or in a Wall Street office, the snappy tunes from *Saturday Night Fever* playing on the radio— and the flood of disco songs that followed in the movie's wake—put a strut in the walk of many a Tony Manero wannabe. Newspapers and magazines featured photos of celebrities stepping out for a night (and not only Saturday nights) at Studio 54—Cher! Farrah! Brooke! Breathless gossip titillated the American public, giving disco a glamorous new allure.

Disco had finally burst into the mainstream. Suddenly disco music was everywhere. Young and old alike sported the "disco look," bought the records, grooved on the energy of the music, and found the release they sought in the thousands of discotheques that sprang up in big cities and small towns throughout the country. Writing in *Esquire* in June 1978, Albert Goldman noted, "In just one short year, disco has exploded from an underground scene down on the New York waterfront or out in the heavily ethnic nabes of Brooklyn and the Bronx into a vast international entertainment industry. Today, disco is right up there with spectator sports and tennis and skiing as one of the ideally contemporary forms of recreation." But disco was a distinctly participatory sport: "Don't be a drag . . . participate," as Chic put it in "Good Times."

Suddenly all sorts of people were joining the team who

only a year earlier would have mocked disco music, the disco scene, and those who actually liked them. Even disco dancing was changing to a more freestyle approach, replacing the choreographed dances like the hustle. Now, anyone able to move to the beat could be part of what *Time* described as disco's "Cinderella world of self-stardom."

Disco provided a chance to escape life's problems and even experience a physical catharsis. Whether it was an actual answer or merely an escape from the questions, the disco scene provided what many, many people wanted. Filling the emotional and spiritual chasm in the heart of America that was one of the legacies of the turbulent sixties, nostalgia for "lost innocence" was a major theme of the seventies (as it has been a recurring theme in American history). The 1950s were revived in romanticized images as a time when Americans seemed surer of themselves, of one another, and of their country. High school kids twisted to the soundtrack of *American Graffiti* and emulated the ever-cool Fonz in TV's *Happy Days.* Parents sighed wistfully for their own young days. But the new beat for the feet was disco. The young and not-so-young alike found their feet shifting, their fingers snapping, to the disco beat.

In the Me Decade, Americans were less inclined to look to traditional sources for meaning and fulfillment, seeking instead to find their own tailor-made answers. Cults and religious groups promising "personal" salvation flourished. Drug use proliferated. What was called the Sexual Revolution increased casual couplings as people sought connection and pleasure in intimate relations. Of course, there were unexpected side effects, such as the skyrocketing rates of sexually transmitted diseases in the seventies.

Together with the decade's economic uncertainties, the

hunger for meaning and personal fulfillment made many Americans receptive to almost anyone or anything that offered answers. Popular culture seemed for many to do precisely that. If one was feeling weighed down by his or her circumstances, the opportunity to get lost in a festive crowd at a disco was very appealing indeed. Like the black artists who made jump blues in the 1940s to give people an outlet for their Depression-related woes, disco also offered at least a temporary escape. Rather than being "the last word in Roman decadence," as the disco scene was often characterized, Albert Goldman pointed out that it was "merely the latest manifestation of the new dispensation."

With a population trying to make sense of their lives and looking to popular culture for answers, it's hard to overstate the role of *Saturday Night Fever* and disco-dancing celebrities in igniting the disco inferno that swept the middle-class masses at the end of the seventies. *Saturday Night Fever* offered something for everyone. *Billboard*'s Radcliffe Joe explained, "For older viewers it brought back many fond memories of the 1950s era of rock and roll, of the twist and Elvis Presley, of slicked back hair and black leather jackets and the occasional rumble in the dark alleyway behind the schoolhouse or down near the docks, and of the first hesitant, fumbling sexual experiments in the rumble seat of the old Ford." Young people found their own lives reflected in the movie's lead characters. Whether laboring in dead-end jobs, like Tony Manero, or working themselves nearly to death in high-powered careers, these people relished their weekly chance to cut loose on a Saturday night.

In New York, the spiritual hub of the disco world, Studio 54 continued going strong a year after its opening. The frolicking famous captured the attention of Americans yearning for a bit of glamour and something more exciting than their own workaday lives. Studio 54 capitalized on the cult of celebrity that took firm hold of America in the seventies. Following in the path that *People* magazine and gossip columnists like Liz Smith had blazed, both beginning in 1974, Studio 54 thrived on the glitter, gossip, and reflected glory that went with its handpicked clientele. Whether among those hanging outside the disco's velvet rope hoping for a glimpse of the blessed who were let in, or perusing the celebrity pictures blanketing the nation's periodicals, voyeurism and vicarious living had become national pastimes.

Nineteen seventy-eight, the hottest year in disco, opened with Donna Summer's new two-disk, four-"act" concept album *Once Upon a Time* being hailed by *Rolling Stone* as perhaps "the ne plus ultra of disco albums." The "eroticized space music" was "another technological triumph for Munich-based producers Giorgio Moroder and Pete Bellotte." As for the "chameleon-voiced" songstress herself, the magazine said Summer "emerges as both the Diana Ross and the Bette Midler of disco and as one of pop culture's all-time camp divas." Featuring Summer on the cover, the March 23, 1978, issue of the ten-year-old rock and roll magazine asked in the headline, "Is There Life After Disco?"

By then, the soundtrack of *Saturday Night Fever* had bumped Fleetwood Mac's *Rumours* from its thirty-three-week reign in the top slot as the nation's number-one album. "None of us expected it to be so big," said Maurice Gibb of the Bee Gees, who wrote seven of the album's songs and performed six of them. Each day, from 175,000 to 200,000 *Saturday Night Fever* eight-tracks, cassettes, and LPs were being sold across the country, according to Al Coury, president of RSO Records.

The Bee Gees were everywhere, suddenly the world's most famous disco artists.

The trio of Barry Gibb and twin brothers Robin and Maurice Gibb had been known as the Brothers Gibb before shortening their name to the Bee Gees. They started out lip-synching rock and roll hits on the Saturday *Gaumont Show* in Manchester, England, in 1956. Two years later, the Gibb family moved to Australia, where the brothers released their first single, "Three Kisses of Love," in 1963. The group's growing popularity led them back to England in 1967. That year they also signed with RSO and had their first hit across the Atlantic, "New York Mining Disaster 1941," a song about the Aberfan mining disaster that killed more than two hundred children in Wales.

By the early 1970s, the Bee Gees were at a low because of the decline in popularity of their style of soft rock. But in 1975, a new R & B and disco sound on the songs "Jive Talkin' " and "Nights on Broadway," from their album *Main Course,* made them major hits. In 1977, four songs written and/or performed by the Bee Gees—"(Love Is) Thicker Than Water," "Emotion," "Stayin' Alive," and "Night Fever"—ranked in the top five slots on *Billboard*'s Hot 100 Chart, something only the Beatles had ever done before. Reviewing the *Saturday Night Fever* soundtrack in *Rolling Stone* in March 1978, Susin Shapiro said, "The Bee Gees have everything going for them: lyrics that don't insult, a band that can open up and utilize each and every electric and/or acoustic possibility without sounding overproduced, great harmonies, and superb dance music." She added that the single " 'You Should Be Dancing' comes as close to disco perfection as anything I've yet heard save for Harold Melvin and the Blue Notes' 'Bad Luck' and LaBelle's 'Lady Marmalade.' "

With increased radio play for the singles from the movie and other disco tunes, the public's appetite for disco music, the fun of the discotheques, and celebrity gawking seemed insatiable. At Studio 54, it became "Every Night Fever," as *Macleans* put it. Continuing to grab headlines, the club in the spring of 1978 hosted Elizabeth Taylor's forty-sixth-birthday party. Rita Christopher reported that the "luminaries in attendance" included Lauren Bacall, *Washington Post* publisher Katherine Graham, Truman Capote, President Nixon's literary agent Irving (Swifty) Lazar, "and naturally, the reigning royalty of Studio 54, [fashion designer] Halston, [Andy] Warhol, Bianca [Jagger], and Margaret Trudeau," the jet-setting wife of Canadian Prime Minister Pierre Trudeau. Taylor's then-husband, U.S. Representative and future senator John Warner of Virginia, didn't attend. Taylor herself may not have noticed his absence, though. One of her entourage explained at the party, "They've been drinking big and I think she's really too high."

Expectations for disco's even bigger success were also running high, stimulated by all the sudden attention to the music, the clubs, the good times to be had, and the money to be made. Radcliffe Joe offered his own forecast for the disco scene in 1978, the year he called "the fourth anniversary of the reactivation of America's romance with discos." He praised the "flexibility" of the new disco format, evidenced by the willingness to change of writers, composers, producers, artists, club owners, and even equipment manufacturers. Joe said that "the escalating involvement of the financial community" as well as the willingness of "internationally recognized personalities" to support the concept made it unlikely that disco would "go the way of the hula hoop and the pet rock" anytime soon.

Internationally recognized personalities weren't the only

ones who had caught the fever. *Billboard* estimated that in 1978, thirty-six million Americans stepped out at one or another of the country's twenty thousand discos. Disco was everywhere, from disco proms to disco cruises to a Dubuque, Iowa, club offering a disco wedding service complete with a smoke machine and light effects. With billions of dollars being generated, specialty publications, its own music charts, and savvy marketers trying to push disco into every American home, Albert Goldman noted that "the new beat for the feet is sending up all the familiar signals that betoken a new wave of mass culture."

The cultural wave became a tsunami once radio and television got seriously involved in 1978. Like other trends in American popular culture in the age of the airwaves, the broadcast media provided literal channels through which disco was pumped into the mainstream. *Billboard* noted that 1978 "was the year disco became legitimate in the eyes of the media."

Radio was slow to embrace disco music until it saw the chance to capitalize on the public's new hunger for 125-beat-per-minute tunes. Hillary Rosen, president of the Recording Industry Association of America, says, "Radio in general is full of small-minded people with limited scope. They have a problem with anything that sounds a little different from the formula. The playlists are very tightly controlled and extraordinarily difficult to get into. [But] every once in a while, radio does respond to consumer demand."

With the surging popularity of disco music, radio finally responded. After years of avoiding disco music in any larger quantity than the few hits that crossed over to the pop charts, radio stations across the country embraced disco in late 1978 and early 1979 after one New York station struck gold with an all-disco format. WKTU-FM was a New York City "mellow rock" station on the verge of bankruptcy, with a paltry 1.3 percent share of the area's listening audience. With a bit of surgery from "radio doctor" Kent Burkhart in the summer of 1978, the station switched to an all-disco format.

WKTU-FM was quickly catapulted to the top of the Arbitron charts, becoming the most listened-to station in the U.S. Within weeks, almost every station in the country with flagging ratings was shifting to a disco format. Doug Hall, *Billboard's* radio and TV programming editor at the time, noted, "Disco is rolling across radio, pushing aside other formats in an upheaval perhaps not seen since the Top 40 came on the scene more than twenty years ago."

Throughout the country, disco was suddenly the hottest thing on the airwaves. Among the growing number of all-disco stations were KSFX-FM in San Francisco, KXYZ-AM in Houston, WBDS-FM in Boston, WSDO-FM in Fort Lauderdale, Florida, and KBOW-AM and KBQQ-FM in Terre Haute, Indiana. Wolfman Jack, the radio jock whose gravelly voice had been introducing pop hits to listeners since the 1950s, was howling about disco in "Wolfman Jack's Disco Party." In what discophiles saw as the clearest sign of the format's power, New York's WABC-AM in early 1979 virtually dismantled its twenty-year-old contemporary-hits format to go disco. The station was even breaking new records in the New York market.

As a teenager in New Jersey, Bernie Lopez, the man behind the Internet's best disco Web site (discomusic.com), listened to WKTU-FM after it switched to disco. "My discovering it one day was like a sort of coming-of-age experience," says Lopez. "I recall that at the time I always had a portable radio with me wherever I went. I was just getting fed up with WABC's shit when I was surfing the dial and heard this music that just kept me tuned in." Like many others, Lopez says he was "actually a little embarrassed that I liked it." But he kept going back to the station. "I would turn back to the other stations, but I always came back. By the end of that fateful day, I was a disco music lover."

Radio wasn't the only broadcast medium to capitalize on the disco craze. On national television, talk-show hosts Merv Griffin and Dinah Shore were at the forefront of those who understood disco's potential and championed it. Griffin's interest in particular led to the nationally televised weekly disco dance contest *Dance Fever,* which he produced in association with Twentieth Century Fox Productions. Bob Murphy, producer of *The Merv Griffin Show,* was excited about disco-on-the-air. "The whole world's gone crazy over disco," he said. "It is unbelievable. Even people in their sixties have told us that *Dance Fever* was one of the best shows ever aired on television."

Other syndicated network shows such as *Midnight Special, Soul Train,* and *American Bandstand* featured disco music. Network television was struck hard by disco fever during the summer and fall of 1978. NBC was the first to climb on the disco bandwagon with *Le Disco,* hosted by none other than *American Bandstand*'s Dick Clark. The show featured the Spinners, the Village People, and a segment taped at Studio 54. CBS's *60 Minutes* devoted an entire segment to disco. CBS also remade the previous year's *Disco '77* into *Disco Magic,* a two-episode special with live acts such as the Village People, Evelyn "Champagne" King, Jimmy "Bo" Horne, and Enchantment. Earlier guests had included the Trammps, the Spinners, Lou Rawls, Silver Convention, Linda Clifford, Odyssey, Vicki Sue Robinson, and Al Green. In the works were episodes with Andy

Gibb, Samantha Sang, and the Average White Band. Patrons at the Fort Lauderdale discotheque where the show was filmed provided the show's "live" atmosphere.

Even the venerable children's show *Sesame Street* had caught the fever. In 1978, the Cookie Monster, Oscar the Grouch, Big Bird, and the other *Sesame Street* characters cut their own disco album. Andy Gibb, younger brother of the Bee Gees, helped out on *Sesame Street Fever.* Because the show had brought so much pleasure to him and his children, Gibb waived his performance fee and asked only that his kids be allowed to meet the *Sesame Street* bunch. Joining forces with "Ice Follies" and "Holiday on Ice," *Sesame Street* promoted its disco album through children's institutions, playgrounds, and shopping centers throughout the country.

Advertising agencies discovered that disco music could boost the sales of just about anything. Most discofied ads were aired on network television, and many used a disco setting to appeal to the clientele being solicited. The products being touted to the disco beat included Prell and Breck shampoos, Trident chewing gum, Burger King fast food, Colt 45, and Sanyo audio and video equipment. The nation's top ad agencies freely admitted they were taking advantage of the public's seemingly incurable disco fever. "There is really nothing new in what we're doing," said Roy Eaton, vice president and director of music at the leading agency Benton & Bowles. "We always make the best possible use of current music trends and disco is what is current."

Thanks to the cultural inundation of disco, club culture provided many of the defining images of the 1970s, from platform shoes to mirror balls. At the heart of the disco phenomenon, though, was the music. In a short time it had come out of the clubs and become the soundtrack of American life at the end of the decade.

THE GROOVE LINE

The sassy urban sound of disco music rocked out of American cities where black men and women made funk, soul, and R & B music, the musical foundations of the new genre. Unlike other shifts in American popular music in the twentieth century that were inspired by black music, disco music remained fundamentally "black." Of course there were also white singers and groups who performed disco music, none more famous—or infamous, in the eyes of some—than the Bee Gees. But most of the genre's best-known musicians were in fact black.

Along with everyone else making disco music, black performers benefited from the boom of interest in disco because of *Saturday Night Fever* and its soundtrack. In 1978, *Billboard* reported that black studio musicians, producers such as Van McCoy and Norman Harris, songwriters and composers, technical and managerial professionals, and of course performers, were in extraordinary demand as the recording and entertainment industries tried to keep up with the surge in demand for disco music. Cities like New York, Los Angeles, Miami, and Philadelphia were hopping with the creative energy of black music makers, whether behind the scenes or onstage in live acts that were increasingly in demand by the disco-craving public.

Individual artists and groups alike were riding high on the wave of success and affluence that comes with selling lots of records. By 1978, Philadelphia International Records—source and sustainer of the Philadelphia Sound—had become the nation's fifth-largest black-owned corporation, annually grossing twenty-five million dollars. Black soloists like Donna Summer, Gloria Gaynor, Barbara Pennington, George McCrae, and Thelma Houston and groups like the Trammps, First Choice, and Crown Heights Affair all enjoyed success because of disco. As Kathie Sledge, of Sister Sledge, said, "To me, disco music opens doors for a lot of acts that were stuck in one category."

That isn't to say they were all happy about "needing" to use disco music to make a name for themselves. Even Donna Summer, the biggest star of the disco era, complained, "You have to sell yourself cheap." Born LaDonna Andre Gaines in Boston on New Year's Eve 1949, Summer got her start at age eighteen singing at Boston's Psychedelic Supermarket with a group called Crow—"the crow being me," said Summer, "because I was the only black member of the group." In 1968 she replaced another future disco diva, Melba Moore, in a German production of the Broadway hit *Hair*. After a stint with the Viennese cast of the show and with the Vienna Folk Opera, Summer returned to Germany. There she performed in productions of *Godspell, Porgy and Bess, Show Boat,* and *The Me Nobody Knows*. She also married Austrian actor Helmut Sommer, whom she left after she hit it big, taking with her a slightly altered version of her ex-husband's last name.

In 1975, Summer got her big break when Munich producers Giorgio Moroder and Pete Bellotte created her springboard to the stars—and permanently altered disco music—with the introduction of the electronic sound known as Euro-disco in Summer's megahit "Love to Love You Baby." The song's twenty-two simulated orgasms caused quite a stir in the U.S. It was banned by the BBC in Britain. The album swiftly went gold.

Two more gold albums followed in 1976, *A Love Trilogy* and *Four Seasons of Love.* In 1977, "I Feel Love," from *I Remember Yesterday,* peaked at number six.

Summer assumed the throne as the uncontested disco queen in 1978 with her starring role in *Thank God It's Friday.* A year later *Bad Girls* was released, rising quickly to number one. Critics hailed the album as the best fusion of rock and disco to date. *Rolling Stone* said that despite "ultraschlock ballads and side two's erratic rock-disco cuts," it "still ranks as the only great disco album other than *Saturday Night Fever.*" Summer appeared on the cover of *Newsweek* in April 1979 with the headline "Disco Takes Over." In June of that year, Summer set a record as the first solo entertainer to hold two of the three top positions on the singles chart simultaneously, with "Hot Stuff" and "Bad Girls."

Because of the crossover appeal of disco, new songs by black artists were played as readily at white clubs as at black ones. One of them was Gloria Gaynor's "I Will Survive." By a poll of deejays, Gaynor had been crowned "Queen of the Discos" back in 1975 after her number-nine remake of the Jackson 5's "Never Can Say Goodbye." But it was her hit "I Will Survive" in 1978 that gave the world a disco anthem that would live on. This B side of a single was Gaynor's personal song of determination after having just lost her mother and had back surgery. The song was broken out in Studio 54, and it went all the way to number one.

Besides bringing attention to disco music in general, the music from the soundtrack of *Saturday Night Fever* was hugely popular in 1978. Individual cuts from the movie were played over and over on radio stations across the country. Four of them reached number one. Not only did the hits from the movie get people to admit they liked disco music, but the music appealed to people of every age. From "teens who ordinarily buy singles to oldsters who never buy pop albums," *Billboard* reported that *Fever* had brought a flood of consumers into record stores and resulted in sales of other music as well. In Miami, Joe Holderness of North Dade Record Land said, "We're getting a lot of elderly people from the condominiums who say they love to hustle." Herb Denne of Minneapolis Music Land said that the Bee Gees' "Stayin' Alive" resonated with older people. "The demographics are amazing," said Rick Saint of Los Angeles's Westwood Wherehouse. "We get kids, the Beverly Hills type, all age groups."

By April 1978, the *Saturday Night Fever* soundtrack was outselling its nearest competitor, Billy Joel's *The Stranger,* by three to one. With the ascendence of "Night Fever" to the number-one slot, the Bee Gees the previous month had become the first act to reach number one with three consecutive single releases since the Jackson 5 had four number-one hits in a row in 1970. The Bee Gees were now tied with Elton John for having the most—six—number-one singles in the 1970s. Beatles veteran Paul McCartney and Stevie Wonder were tied in second place, with five each.

In the summer of 1978, the prime of disco's life at center stage, disco acts were crossing over into the nation's pop charts, giving exposure to disco artists far beyond their original dance-floor fans and generating substantial album sales. Among those enjoying this crossover success were Evelyn "Champagne" King, A Taste of Honey, and Rick James. Larkin Arnold, vice president and general manager of Capitol Records' soul music division, said the *Saturday Night Fever* soundtrack had "spread disco music to Middle America." He added, "It's conducive to tunes like 'Runaway Love,' 'Shame,' and 'Boogie Oogie Oogie.' That's why they're happening pop."

After breaking out in the New York market in April, radio play helped A Taste of Honey's "Boogie Oogie Oogie" spread throughout the Northeast. The single was perhaps destined to succeed after Capitol hired a psychic to draw up an astrological chart for the song based on its time and place of recording. "Runaway Love" had an advantage in that singer Linda Clifford had already charted with "If My Friends Could See Me Now" and "Gypsy Lady." Originally released in September 1977, Evelyn "Champagne" King's "Shame" took more than nine months to rise to the top. Starting in Boston, the single spread down the East Coast—and became RCA's top-selling twelve-inch disco disc, with upwards of one million copies sold.

Producer T. (Theodore) Life had heard Evelyn King singing as she cleaned the rest rooms at the Philadelphia International Records offices, and told her, "One day I'm going to make you a star, young lady." King thought, "Yeah, I've heard that before." She was only eighteen years old when "Shame" hit number one on the disco chart in 1978. She said she was known as "Bubbles" because "I used to blow spit bubbles at people." With one of the best voices in disco, King prided herself on being able to sing "men's way," imitating Isaac Hayes and Barry White. *Rolling Stone* said "her vocal range extends from a kittenish soprano to a fog-horn baritone."

From its roots in rhythm and blues, disco's fast-spreading tendrils wrapped around virtually every other style of music—including country, classical, pop, rock, even Broadway show tunes. Artists such as Barbra Streisand, Cher, Andy Williams, Shirley Bassey, and Dolly Parton recorded disco songs. Diana Ross had immediately become a disco diva with her smash

1976 hit "Love Hangover." Four years later, Ross would have two number-one disco hits, "I'm Coming Out" (a gay anthem to this day) and "Upside Down."

The rock band Wild Cherry learned that patrons at the 2001 disco in Pittsburgh were more interested in a good time than in their brand of aggressive rock, and the band threw back the taunts they received in their number-one hit "Play That Funky Music." The most famous rockers to hit disco pay dirt were as surprised by their success as their fans were surprised that they had "stooped" to disco when the Rolling Stones hit the top with their 1978 hit "Miss You." The group's manager had added a disco beat to the song without telling them. Whatever irritation they may have felt was surely mollified by the cool green stuff that flows from a hit song.

By 1979, *Newsweek* was reporting "Record companies now urge new acts to include at least one disco cut on their albums as a way of getting radio exposure." Even old-timers were cashing in on the disco craze. Legendary bluesman B. B. King defended his own foray into disco, saying "I think in terms of survival." Swing and jazz great Cab Calloway recorded a disco version of his standard "Minnie the Mooch," and even developed a disco dance to complement the tune. Ethel "There's No Business Like Show Business" Merman recorded a disco album featuring thumped-up show tunes, including Cole Porter's "I Get a Kick Out of You" and Irving Berlin's "Alexander's Ragtime Band." She hoped the album would appeal to teenagers and revive interest in show music. Said Merman, "I am just as enthused about this album as I was about my first job, and I don't care if people accuse me of jumping on the disco bandwagon."

That bandwagon rolled on to wealth and lavish praise

within the recording industry. Half of *Billboard*'s 1978 year-end selection of "artists of the year" were disco-related. The influential trade magazine selected the soundtrack of *Saturday Night Fever* as the album and soundtrack of the year. By that point it had become the bestselling album in the history of recorded music, with sales approaching thirty million copies. No one was surprised when Donna Summer was picked disco artist of the year. The Bee Gees were picked the group of the year. Brother Andy had the year's top single ("Shadow Dancing"). And disco-making Earth, Wind & Fire were collectively named soul artist of the year.

Even rock-loving *Rolling Stone* picked the Bee Gees' "Stayin' Alive" as the top single of 1978. The brothers also shared the *Rolling Stone* 1978 Critics Award for producers of the year because of their work on "all their hit singles," as the magazine put it. These awards had special significance because *Rolling Stone* was never fond of disco music. Its tentative embrace of the genre was evident in a year-end review of Donna Summer's *Live and More,* released in September 1978. The album included the number-one hits "MacArthur Park," "Last Dance" from *Thank God It's Friday,* and "Heaven Knows"—three of Summer's best-known and most successful songs. Tom Carson's review said, "If disco weren't such a limiting genre, Donna Summer might have already been recognized as the Diana Ross of the Seventies." He praised her "fine, dramatic voice, immense charm, and unusually tasteful technical control." Like Ross, he noted, Summer had what he described as "an erotic, bitchy sullenness, perpetually threatening to break through the slick pop surface of her music." But because she was seen as a disco act, Summer's superstardom was dismissed.

Despite the condescension of rock critics, the disco music

of 1978 cleaned up at Grammy Awards time in the winter of 1979. The recording industry's most prestigious awards heaped yet more praise on the soundtrack of *Saturday Night Fever*, naming it album of the year—the first time a soundtrack ever had that distinction. Billy Joel's "Just the Way You Are" took the Grammy for record of the year, though the Bee Gees were expected to win the award. Still, the group managed to take away no less than five Grammys, including best vocal arrangement for "Stayin' Alive" and best pop group for the second year in a row. They were the first group to repeat that particular award since the Carpenters had done it in 1970–71.

In addition to the Bee Gees, disco was well represented in the Grammys. Donna Summer won for best R & B female vocal performance for "Last Dance," which itself was named best R & B song of the year. Paul Jabara won the Grammy for writing the song—and later that spring won an Academy Award for best original song for a movie, too. Earth, Wind & Fire won for vocal performance by a duo, group, or chorus, and a second time for instrumental performance on "Runnin.'" Even crooner Barry Manilow was able to land the Grammy that year for best pop male vocal performance for his disco hit "Copacabana (At the Copa)."

In comparison to the disheveled state of rock music at the time, disco was the smart young upstart. It was evident in A Taste of Honey beating out the Cars and Elvis Costello for the Grammys' artist of the year—a first for a black group. For three years in a row, the award had been given to a group with mass appeal and one giant single over one with more album "credibility." Rockers were in high dudgeon, especially after Debby "You Light Up My Life" Boone had actually beat out Foreigner the year before for the best new artist award.

With all this exposure and popularity, disco was bound to change. And change it did, quite rapidly. "There are more trends in disco than you can shake your booty at this year," noted Dick Nusser in *Billboard* in early 1979, looking back at what had been disco's best year. The music was picking up speed, now flicking along at a hot and bothered 142 beats per minute. The songs were longer, with deejays stretching eight-minute cuts into sixteen-minute extravaganzas. The music was more sophisticated, incorporating the synthesized sounds of Europe, particularly Germany. Nusser noted that even lyrics were packing a new punch in songs like "Shame," Cheryl Lynn's "Got to Be Real," and Gloria Gaynor's "I Will Survive."

There had not been an explosion into the mainstream of such musical magnitude since the birth of rock and roll itself in the 1950s. Nusser wasn't the only one in 1978 who believed that "at the rate disco is changing, expanding, and becoming diversified, there should be no doubt that it can no longer be considered a passing fad."

I LOVE THE NIGHTLIFE

Nowhere was the disco fad played out more completely than in the discotheques themselves. Albert Goldman called them "psychedelic country clubs." Dressed in clothing spun from the imaginations of laboratory scientists, clubgoers sniffed, snorted, smoked, sweated, and strutted the nights away under the twirling lights, in the fog. In 1978, new discotheques were opening everywhere a patch of dance floor could be found, in big cities and small towns alike. As the year got under way, Radcliffe Joe reported in *Billboard* that cities like Los Angeles, Miami, Chicago, Dallas, Houston, and New

Orleans were gearing up to challenge the Big Apple "for the enviable distinction of being the disco capital of the nation."

Los Angeles ranked second to New York, with only eight major clubs catering to the disco needs of the city's five-million-plus who might like some entertainment. But with new clubs opening all over the city, two major radio stations broadcasting disco music, and the growing support of the press—always eager to support a hot new trend in ever-trendy L.A.—the City of Angels was seen as gaining on New York for the title of number-one disco city in the U.S.

By the middle of 1978, a dozen new dance clubs had opened in San Francisco in as many months, and more were opening each week. Besides the new places, existing discos were remodeled, bars that featured live rock turned to recorded disco, and dance schools and classes swelled in size. The largest club in the city was one-year-old Trocadero Transfer, with its four-thousand-square-foot dance floor. Like Studio 54, Trocadero was located in an old television studio building. Also like 54, it was a membership club, costing seventy-five dollars a year plus a five-dollar weekend cover charge. Non-members were slapped with a "staggering" (as Radcliffe Joe put it at the time) fifteen-dollar cover on weekends.

San Francisco's best-known disco was the City. The club featured 2,450 watts of sound power and a forty-thousand-dollar lighting system, whose centerpiece was a massive crown—with one thousand, six hundred bulbs, run by a matrix control system—suspended above the middle of the dance floor. With the latter-day gold rush of disco, the three-and-a-half-year-old City had seen its business increase exponentially. Since *Saturday Night Fever* opened, City's owner, Tom Sanford, said the club's Monday night disco-dance classes had grown from an average of forty to eighty, to upwards of two hundred students. The City was the site of the party for the world premiere of *Thank God It's Friday* on May 19, 1978, hosted by Casablanca Records, for more than six hundred guests.

Although those looking back at the seventies disco era have focused almost exclusively on the "celebrity discos," like Studio 54, the fact is that there was an assortment of clubs for every taste, persuasion, and pocketbook. For those who wanted the effects of the disco without ever leaving home, mail-order gift houses sold home disco kits for several thousand dollars. But the most exciting aspect of disco was the disco scene, the clubs themselves. Investors and owners were equally excited by the potential profits of running a discotheque. Los Angeles lawyer David Kenner, the lead investor in a disco called Dillon's, told *Business Week* in June 1978 that a 40 percent return was possible and an initial investment could be recouped within a year. The magazine noted, "The promise of such quick cash is fueling a coast-to-coast explosion of what originally was a European idea—'le disco.' "

In Buffalo, a Boeing 747 jetliner, situated appropriately across the street from Greater Buffalo International Airport, was the setting for that snowy city's Club 747. Not only was the club popular among the locals, but owner Jim Cosentino planned to take the concept national. In the summer of 1978, he was negotiating leases for Club 747s in Pittsburgh and Fort Lauderdale, and looking at Houston, Boston, Cincinnati, and even Japan.

Chicago's Nimbus, among the country's most elaborate clubs, opened in November 1978. Located in the far south suburb of Dolton, Illinois, it featured one of the Midwest's largest dance floors, an elaborate lighting system, and a nimbus cloud theme carried out in a carpet mural on three walls surrounding one of the bars. By 1978 New Orleans' Parade was already three years old. Named after the city's famous Mardi Gras parade, the club's office manager, Claudia Speicher, attributed its longevity—it was New Orleans' longest-surviving disco at that point—to constantly renovating its sound system and featuring the most spectacular light show in town.

In Spartanburg, South Carolina, it was the plush new seventeen-thousand-square-foot "Irish pub" disco called O'Sullivan's. Skip Corn, the deejay there, said it was hard for Carolina residents to become "disco-music-oriented" because "few radio stations in the area are willing to program any sort of uptempo music." But area club owners gave deejays almost total control. Plugged into the national music scene, the spinners brought disco to yet another region. Nearly one thousand disco-deprived Carolinians danced the nights away to Corn's well-mixed tunes at O'Sullivan's. Thanks to the deejays' efforts, Corn said he was sure the disco concept in the Carolinas had passed the fad stage and was now a big business for area entrepreneurs. "What is happening," he told *Billboard*, "is that the Manhattan-style club is no longer something we hear about down here. It has become a reality."

Since the early years of discotheques, Régine Zylberberg's personal reality was the world of night people. She was also used to being in the vanguard of an international trend. It was, after all, in her original Parisian nightclub, Chez Régine, that the twist—the last international dance craze before disco—had been introduced to Europe in 1960. Celebrating her quarter-century as the self-proclaimed "queen of the night," Régine opened her tenth club in 1978, a blue art deco room in Montreal's new Hyatt Regency hotel. The club was estimated to have cost more than a million dollars. The annual membership fee was $350, and cocktails cost $3.50 each.

Even the federal government in 1978 managed to shake its own substantial booty to the disco beat. The Buck Stops Here, a fitting name for a Washington disco that opened that year, was paid for with $750,000 in federal funds. Located in the building that housed the Federal Home Loan Bank Board, the "total concept" establishment was an employee cafeteria by day, a cocktail bar in the early evening featuring music of the 1930s and 1940s, and a restaurant and disco later at night. Since this was button-down Washington, Mike O'Harro, owner of the popular D.C. club Tramps and a consultant to the project, said, "We're looking for a more staid, more sophisticated crowd than the usual disco audience—people who have money to spend."

Hotels, motels, and restaurants weren't about to miss the opportunity presented by disco's sudden popularity. Ramada Inns, with five hundred franchised hotels and 112 wholly owned inns, planned to put a disco in all of its hotels. The Hilton Hotel chain also was looking into adding discotheques as part of its hotel facilities.

Disco franchises were offered as early as 1974–75 by the soon-defunct Dimples chain. But the formation of what became the nation's two largest disco franchisers—Pittsburgh-based 2001 Clubs of America and Murray the K's Discos on Wheels, a New York–based mobile-disco franchiser—really set the concept in motion. The average 2001 franchise required an initial investment of about half a million dollars, in addition to more than a million dollars to put the club together and a thirty-five-thousand-dollar franchise fee. As if those expenses weren't enough, 2001 also took 5 percent of the franchise gross and another 1 percent for cooperative advertising. Franchisers tended to locate their clubs outside the cities because of competition from independently owned clubs in major urban areas. Space also was an important consideration, as 2001 clubs typically were huge—between twenty thousand and thirty thousand square feet.

Creating a disco that would draw crowds and make money was a complex and expensive undertaking. But as Studio 54's owners had found, the investment could be earned back pretty quickly. According to *Nation's Business,* in 1979 an average small disco spent between eight and fifteen thousand dollars for a lighting system. The kind of lighted dance floors that became associated with disco dancing cost close to eighteen thousand dollars—excluding installation—for a sixteen-by-thirty-two-foot floor.

Five years after Culver City, California, sound and lighting company Wavelength, Inc., got into the disco business, company president Brian Edwards in 1978 said, "Now, things are speeding up, and clubs are asking for more complex equipment." One of Wavelength's biggest jobs, turning the old Hollywood Palace in Los Angeles into a disco, would run close to one million dollars. In the meantime, Edwards said the company's best business was in the Midwest and South. They were also contracted to equip discos in Switzerland and Australia. Edwards said the company doubled its business in 1978, and expected another 50 percent increase in 1979. Among its most popular items were four-hundred-dollar fog-making machines and ninety-dollar mirror balls.

As bastions of the latest in audio and video technology, it was natural the discos would also pioneer the videodisc—as popular today as it was predicted to become when it premiered in the seventies. The Mad Hatter, in Tampa, Florida, was one of the earliest discos to offer the TV generation the ultimate audiovisual disco experience when it installed a videodisc system that recorded the action on the dance floor and then projected it on to the walls of the disco in images that were sixteen feet wide and ten feet high. The fantasy of so many disco dancers to be the star of their own disco movie could be realized thanks to laser discs, and mugging for the cameras became a regular part of the scene at the clubs that installed similar systems.

After its introduction at the Empire Rollerdome in Brooklyn, New York, other roller rinks throughout the country soon caught on to what was called roller disco. Cher was reported to be so excited about roller disco that she added the track "Hell on Wheels" to her 1979 dance album *Prisoner.* Because the roller discos didn't serve alcohol, roller disco appealed to underage teens and even entire families. Cover charges were lower than at standard discos. Roller disco "dancing" made fitness fun. The money spent by the rinks on sound-system and lighting upgrades made them ready to cash in on the building discomania. Paul Gregory, whose New York company, Lite-Lab, had designed the disco set in *Saturday Night Fever,* said the upgrades in the roller rinks had "sparked a rebirth for skating rinks in every party of the country." Roller disco helped save the nation's estimated five thousand roller rinks, in decline since their early 1960s heyday.

When the concept of roller disco was introduced, skeptics balked. But then, they had balked at the idea of disco itself. Millions of dollars were pumped into outfitting roller rinks to rival the best discotheques. In Los Angeles, where roller-disco fever was even more acute than in New York, what Radcliffe Joe called "multimillion-dollar roller dance palaces" were springing up. Among them was Flipper's, built in 1978 by former record-industry executive Denny Cordell, attorney Nick Cowan, and a radio personality from Britain called Flipper (not to be confused with the porpoise of the same name featured in the eponymous mid-sixties TV show). State-of-the-art sound and lighting systems became as essential to the roller rinks as knee, shoulder, and elbow pads and protective headgear were essential to skater/dancers.

Roller disco caught on even in the heartland. Michael D'Orso, owner of the Colerain Skate Land in Cincinnati, Ohio, said, "Several years ago, rinks were the second-class entertainment of America. Today they've been upgraded to the point where some of the new rinks may cost as much as a million dollars." Roller disco was a welcome change, said D'Orso. "It's slowed the kids down a little, for one thing," he said. "Now they have dance movements for their feet—and they put their own steps together."

Another twist on the roller-disco fun was outdoor roller disco. Dancers could, with a cassette player or radio, turn any pathway or paved driveway into an instant dance floor. When the first portable stereo cassette player came on the market in 1979—Sony's Stowaway, the precursor of the Walkman—roller disco became even more mobile as skater/dancers glided through public parks and streets, privately tuned in to their favorite disco tunes.

The record industry didn't want to repeat its earlier mistake of ignoring disco until it had already become a pop-cultural phenomenon, and it soon recognized the power of the roller rinks to promote new disco music. In 1978, some one thousand, five hundred of the nation's roller rinks banded together to insist that they become record breakers for the music industry. Accommodating more than two thousand skaters at a time, the average roller rink could reach large numbers of potential record buyers. Now roller-rink operators hounded the record companies the way disco deejays had done a few years before in their own efforts to be taken seriously as key promoters of new disco records.

Given the success of the roller discos with young people, enterprising capitalists realized there was money to be made by catering to underage teens. "Dry" clubs like Illusions in Boston, T.G.I. Friday's in Las Vegas, the Ice Factory in Strouds-burg, Pennsylvania, and the Fourth Street Annex in Santa Rosa, California, provided young people with a fun alternative to the hanging-out boredom of teen life. For the California brat pack, Michael Del Rey and David Price of Price–Del Ray Productions created a chain of teen discotheques modeled after Studio 54, complete with the insider-outsider exclusivity. Echoing Steve Rubell's "salad-tossing" philosophy of mixing up a handpicked crowd, Del Rey said, "They don't have to be rich. They merely have to look that way."

While disco entrepreneurs were pulling the crowds into their establishments, mobile-disco operators were doing their bit for the disco fad—as well as for the decade's 1950s nostalgia—with their own version of the record hop. These traveling disco shows could be hired to bring the disco touch to weddings, bar mitzvahs, old-folks' homes, and school auditoriums. A couple hundred dollars would buy a two-hour show that might include some revolving colored bulbs and a small sound system. Two to three thousand dollars bought the works: a four-hour production that included a light show, portable computerized lighted dance floor, fog machines, and state-of-the-art sound equipment. Unlike their counterparts in the clubs, mobile deejays were not highly regarded in the record industry and got few if any promotional copies of new records. For this reason, Radcliffe Joe said the mobile-disco operator was "unable to rid himself of the feeling that he is something of an outcast, of only peripheral importance to the industry to which he contributes so much time, effort, and creativity."

Even as the number and variety of nightspots offering recorded disco-dance music proliferated across the U.S., New York clubs as early as 1978 were turning to live acts, theme parties, and other gimmicky means to counteract the apparent leveling off of the city's own disco boom. Always-cutting-edge Régine's joined the city's growing list of discos offering a mix of live and recorded music—among them, Copacabana, Starship Discovery I, Leviticus, Les Mouches, and Town Hill 2. Ironically, the shift in policy was spurred at least in part by a campaign of Musicians Union Local 802 against discotheques offering only recorded music—the very thing "record libraries" were created to do. Artists featured in the New York clubs included Bette Midler, Gloria Gaynor, the Trammps, Silver Convention, First Choice, Crown Heights Affair, the Andrea True Connection, Sister Sledge, and Harold Melvin and the Blue Notes.

Hurrah's, another fashionable club, hoped its mini-theater production titled *Neon Woman*—featuring well-known female impersonator Divine—would "sustain the interest of its wayward clientele," as Radcliffe Joe put it. Infinity, still another stylish Manhattan nightspot that had inspired Studio 54's owners, offered sexual fantasy parties to spark a bit of heat during the cold winter of 1978. *Billboard* reported, "The general idea behind the concept is to encourage patrons to hang loose and do whatever comes naturally."

With live acts suddenly the new rage in New York discos, it

didn't take long for the concept to catch on throughout the country and at least temporarily change the very nature of what the discotheque was about. Don Johnson, a deejay at the Chateau Disco, said, "It's difficult to expand musically if you don't bring in live artists. Once the newness of a disco wears off, there must be something else to offer the people." The City in San Francisco filled its showroom to the five-hundred-person capacity with such top disco acts as Grace Jones, Tuxedo Junction, and Silver Convention. Don Miley, assistant to owner Tom Sanford, said the City had followed the trend to incorporate live acts that started in New York. "We didn't initially know how adding live entertainment would go over," said Miley. "But when we put Grace Jones in here in February, it went over so well, we had club owners from other states calling us saying they want to book live acts, too."

By 1979 the New York clubs were already swearing off live acts. Club owners had soon learned that the most reasonably priced disco acts were unknowns who couldn't draw the crowds they wanted. Popular and experienced live disco acts were too expensive, or were discouraged by record labels that insisted live disco appearances weren't the way to build large followings (large concert halls were). Club owners also found it easier to program recorded music than to deal with the temperaments of divas and divos. Cerrone, for example, was quoted as saying, "When I perform I don't want people talking or drinking or dancing. I want people to look at Cerrone."

Behind the artists and their egos, behind the music, the clubs, the lights, the fog, and the clothing accessories touted in 1978 as essentials to the disco scene, was an expanding industry comprising a variety of sub-industries suddenly related by marriage in the fusion of disco. From fashion designers to

lighting companies, hordes of savvy moneymakers were dancing what *Business Week* called "the feverish hustle for big disco
profits."

Nearly one thousand, three hundred delegates turned out
for *Billboard*'s fourth disco forum in New York City at the end of
June 1978. The three-day meeting included seminars aimed at
every level of the disco world, from innovations in disco fashions to technology. "[The year] 1978 will long be remembered
as the era when millions of Americans got back on their feet,"
said Casablanca Records president Neil Bogart in the forum's
keynote address. "The disco phenomenon is real," he added. "It
is more than just the sale of millions of records. It is more than
the sound that's sweeping through discos and radio stations all
over the world." And, Bogart predicted, the crest of the disco
wave was yet to come.

News from the forum revealed the hopes and concerns of
all those working behind the scenes to fuel the disco phenomenon. Club owners were quick to point out that a successful club
required "more than light and sound." Club franchisers were so
busy trying to widely replicate the mood and attitude of particular clubs that worried owners feared being tagged in their
local areas as the "Burger Kings of Disco." Deejays were divided
over whether or not to unionize. Complaining that they were
disrespected (and couldn't get demo records), mobile deejays
described their needs and problems. The pluses and minuses
of live acts in the clubs were weighed.

Almost every part of the U.S. was represented at the forum,
including Alaska, Hawaii, and Puerto Rico. Fourteen foreign
countries had delegates there. Ninety-one registrants represented twenty-eight different record labels. Spokespeople from
seventy-two companies occupied more than sixty-three exhibit

hall booths and twenty-four sound rooms. Entertainment for the forum—at Manhattan's hot new club Xenon and taped to air as a TV special—was a who's-who of the biggest disco stars of the day: A Taste of Honey opened with "Searching for Your Love." Next the Trammps filled the dance floor with the sounds of "Disco Inferno." Then it was Tavares performing their own version of *Saturday Night Fever* hit "More Than a Woman." Other artists entertaining the conferees included Donna Summer, Andy Gibb, Linda Clifford, T. Connection, Loleatta Holloway, the Village People, Chic, Peter Brown, and Brooklyn Dreams.

The disco forum was so popular in 1978 that *Billboard* decided to hold it twice a year beginning in 1979. The growing international interest in disco was evident in the suggestion during the forum that a kind of disco cultural exchange be established between the U.S. and Europe. Lest anyone doubt the real origins of disco music and the cultural upheaval it had inspired, France's Alec Costandinos noted in a session devoted to the evolution of pop/disco that there was no such thing as a "disco movement" in Europe. "The energy and power came from the United States," he said.

At the very center of the growing international disco movement emanating from the U.S. were the record companies, now realizing there were big profits to be made on disco music. Going beyond merely appealing to club deejays to play their records, the labels took their ad campaigns directly to the disco-loving public. In January 1978, Salsoul Records—now calling itself "The Disco Music Company"—launched a nationwide "disco awareness program." Its effort to bridge the gap between discotheques, radio, record wholesalers and retailers, and a broad segment of the entertainment-hungry public included T-shirts, countertop displays, buttons, and even a disco handbook aimed at radio station program directors. In magazine ads its message was direct and to the point of disco in general: "Dance Your Ass Off to Salsoul Records." Like other labels, Salsoul also was grooming its disco acts for crossover from the disco charts to the pop charts—where the real money was to be made.

By the end of 1978, disco was a cultural phenomenon international in scope. For the first time, the recording industry acknowledged in a slew of Grammy Awards that something important was going on, that this dance music called disco was just what people seemed to need and want at the tail end of the seventies. Tens of millions of records had by now been sold, and tens of millions of people were making the disco scene. Even television and radio had succumbed, convinced at last by the audience share to be gained from disco-oriented programs.

Disco was on the agenda of the fifty-five hundred attending the thirteenth annual International Music and Publishers Market (MIDEM, from the initials of the French name) in Cannes, France, on January 14, 1979. Among their interests were disco and the takeover of independent U.S. record labels by the majors. "Disco, once the stepchild of the music industry, has come into its own," said *Billboard*. A panel at its fifth disco forum, in February 1979, included representatives of RCA, Atlantic, Polydor, Casablanca, Sam/CBS, TK, and Prelude— among the biggest names in disco record labels. Ray Caviano, executive director of Warner Bros.' disco department and head of his own RFC label, said, "We have finally made the big time." With the increased involvement of the major record companies everyone expected more disco releases and better coordination on the international level so American disco music could be disseminated more efficiently and widely to the entire world.

On April 10, 1979, the National Association of Recording Merchandisers (NARM) reported that nearly one in ten records sold in the U.S. in 1978 was disco-oriented. The following month, the National Academy of Recording Arts and Sciences (NARAS) expanded the Grammy Award categories to include rock, disco, and jazz fusion.

Reflecting disco's arrival at the center of the cultural mainstream, *Billboard,* the recording industry's newspaper of record, accorded what it had called the business of "the discos" the ultimate status in the world of pop culture and celebrity: a one-word name. Beginning in 1979 *Billboard* symbolically changed the name of its own news division covering "the discos" to, simply, "disco." The small shift in language was clear evidence that something more than just a change in popular musical tastes was under way. In fact, an era was being defined.

For a while, during that era, nothing was bigger, more exciting, or more lucrative than disco. Everything it touched turned to gold. Everyone in the entertainment industries wanted some of that gold for themselves. And the American public couldn't seem to get enough.

3

WHAT IT BECAME

For a few years three quarters of the way through history's most violent century, people across the globe shared the joy and peace that participants in the sixties counterculture had dreamed of—at least while they were dancing in the discos. The euphoria that was disco spread as the seventies came to a close. Like a kind of pandemic of pleasure, disco fever literally swept the planet. In Italy it was called *travoltismo* after the sexy young star of *Saturday Night Fever.* Even in China, reported *Newsweek,* a group of Chinese guests at the home of a British embassy official had "celebrated their country's new ties with the U.S. by doing the Peking hustle."

From their beginning, disco music and discotheques themselves united like-minded people in a shared experience of physical exuberance. "Disco," observed *Billboard*'s Radcliffe Joe, "has exhibited an extraordinary ability to bring together people of varying colors, races, ideologies, sexual preferences, and social financial levels in an ecumenical dialogue of music and dance which transcends many of the limitations of petty everyday prejudices."

Something deep, primal, and universal seems to lie behind the need to dance, and disco fulfilled that need in spades. The music's ability to stimulate the body came from the meshing of form and content, pulsing music and sexy lyrics to excite the erotic urge. As journalist Nathan Fain put it, "The lyrics of disco, if that is the term, play on the words dance, love, boogie, get down—not meant to be heard so much as absorbed like the pounding beat behind them."

Many, however, saw the "love" that disco inspired in different terms. Albert Goldman said in a 1978 *Esquire* article that disco culture wasn't about loving another person but love of the self. "Outside the entrance to every discotheque," he wrote, "should be erected a statue to the presiding deity: Narcissus." Whereas sexual desire drives people into one another's arms for the sake of emotional connection and physical release, disco culture drove revelers deeper into themselves.

Disco culture was about pleasure and fun. But its single-minded devotion to "good times," as disco supergroup Chic so memorably called them, meant there was no room in the disco lifestyle for anything that was less than fun or other than personally—and immediately—gratifying. The escape offered in the discos turned into the escapism that pervaded the lifestyle. Anthony Haden-Guest described this pleasure-saturated, chicly exclusive disco scene as "a bizarre, self-absorbed social ecosystem." At the center of it, of course, was the music. Disco performers understood both the sensuality of disco and the Me Decade craving for star status that impelled many club-scene devotees. Nile Rodgers, co-founder of Chic, said disco "was the most hedonistic music I had ever heard in my life. It was really all about Me! Me! Me! Me!"

Commercial disco culture relied on the hedonistic (and narcissistic) appeal of commercial disco music, and the snooty exclusivity of hot discotheques, to remain popular. It was important to keep people coming back to the clubs by making them believe they were "special" for patronizing a particular dance hall. Nowhere was this truer than the place Nathan Fain called the "mother church of international nightlife chic," Studio 54. He explained, "If disco will submit at all to a defining circle, it is this idea of high exclusivity that keeps the sleek and lithe on one side of the velvet rope and the so-called 'bridge and tunnel' people from beyond Manhattan on the other, shouting 'Steve! Steve!' in vain, hoping to win their street audition from Studio 54 owner Steve Rubell."

The trappings of commercial disco culture—the explosion of an underground movement into the mainstream of American popular culture through the print and broadcast media and through the marketplace—are the artifacts of 1970s American popular culture, the images in people's minds when they think of the seventies. It's telling of disco's impact that for so many people "the seventies" and "disco" are indistinguishable. Snapshots of the disco years capture their ephemeral moments of pleasure—the hilarious smiles, coked-out stares, just-sexed (or just-about-to-be) vamps, the sweaty arms thrust exuberantly heavenward, the campy costumes of the revelers. Those images give only a two-dimensional view of what disco was about. Other images from the disco years provide a little more information, including the era's symbols, dances, clothing, and Hollywood movies featuring disco as a theme. It all came together to make disco the biggest popular-culture and musical phenomenon of the final quarter of the last century.

Even in the 1970s nothing was more "seventies" than going to a discotheque. Central to the disco lifestyle were the discos, the places where the music could be heard and party folk could find one another. At the end of the decade, more than one hundred thousand discotheques were operating throughout the world, annually grossing upwards of eight billion dollars. By 1978, thousands of discotheques in the U.S. alone were pumping out the disco sound and offering up a taste of bliss to the millions of Americans who made the disco scene that year.

Studio 54 continued to be "the world's top celebrity disco," as it was widely described. Emphasizing its exclusivity, *Macleans* said, "Acceptance at Studio 54 is tantamount to the ritual anointment that accompanies a coronation." But while most American disco enthusiasts might have liked to dance at Studio 54, the fact is they had to find their pleasure and release closer to home. Even in New York, there were other discos that drained away at least some of Studio's wanna-be crowd and attracted many others who valued a good time and an unpretentious crowd more than they did the abusive treatment too often doled out at the famous club's front door.

"We want the *craziness* of Studio 54 plus the *comfort* of Régine's," said Peppo Vanini, a co-owner with Howard Stein of the two-million-dollar Xenon, just before the club's 1978 opening. But the craziness of getting into one of the club's early parties was anything but comfortable, as Anthony Haden-Guest described it in *New York*. "Getting into the Xenon party was indeed every bit as hellish as one could possibly imagine," he wrote, "a quantum escalation of the pain threshold set by Studio 54. Crowds surged and growled, waving those tiny oblong

cards that denoted extreme importance." Some of the estimated five hundred members of "the Core"—Haden-Guest
described them as "the starriest of disco regulars"—were at the
party, stamping the new disco with their greatly desired
approval.

In his report from the front lines of the escalating competition between Studio 54 and the newer clubs cutting into its
business, Haden-Guest described the Xenon partygoers in a
way that captured the zany seriousness with which Manhattan
celebrity-disco devotees took their nocturnal activities. Among
the opening night's "fashion totems"—"They expect to get in
free, and they get quite angry if they don't," said Xenon co-
owner Howard Stein—were a man wearing black, white gloves,
a bowler, a cane, and a blank mirrored mask, and a Wall Street
captain of industry wearing a flouncy dress, a wedding cake of
a hat, and roller skates. The latter, of course, was New York
nightlife fixture Rollerina.

Still another New York club was drawing a different crowd,
glamorous in its own way but decidedly less affected. In the
summer of 1978, the G. G. Knickerbocker, a club formerly
called the Gilded Grape that had opened in 1974 on the north
side of Forty-fifth Street at Eighth Avenue, opened what it
called the Barnum Room. In a space at the club's rear—it once
housed the Peppermint Lounge—a net was spread above the
heads of the dancers. Overhead, half-naked men and transvestites flew through the air, turning somersaults to the pounding
disco beat.

Just as the twist had transformed the Peppermint Lounge
in the early sixties from a seedy Times Square dive into *the*
place to be, the Barnum Room began within months of its premiere to attract some new faces among its own rough-and-

tumble crowd. The likes of Truman Capote, Robert Redford, Halston, and Andy Warhol were spotted there. Despite the celebrity gawkers, the unusual disco's usual clientele were largely transvestites—prompting *New York* editor Orde Coombs to describe the Barnum Room as "a noisy playground where what you see is not what you get."

Of course there were other discos in New York, the world's disco capital, catering to different tastes and tribal affiliations. There was Leviticus, described by *Ebony* as "the mainstay of black disco dancing in midtown Manhattan." New York New York, a club designed for a more working-class crowd, opened in May 1977. Five months later *The New Yorker* noted that the club was using a "terrific gimmick" to create a "Dr. Frankenstein" atmosphere: fog. Made with dry ice mixed with 160-degree water in fog machines, the steam billowed from five vents, rising and dropping to waist level. "The wetness is agreeable if you are a woman in tights," observed a *New Yorker* commentator, "but it takes the creases out of men's trousers. I noticed one man peering down at himself when the fog had been turned off for a few moments; he was pinching the trouser legs of his safari suit, trying to press the creases back."

Even at disco's peak, *Billboard* estimated that at least 50 percent of the nation's dance clubs were gay. Hot music, an attractive crowd, and enthusiastic dancing were the norm in those clubs. But as Kitty Hanson put it in her 1978 handbook *Disco Fever,* "Invariably, as news about a new gay club with great sound and decor gets around, straight people who want to dance start knocking at the door."

On the West Coast, San Francisco's gay club Trocadero Transfer was widely regarded as one of the best hard-core discos anywhere. One former deejay recalled Trocadero as a place

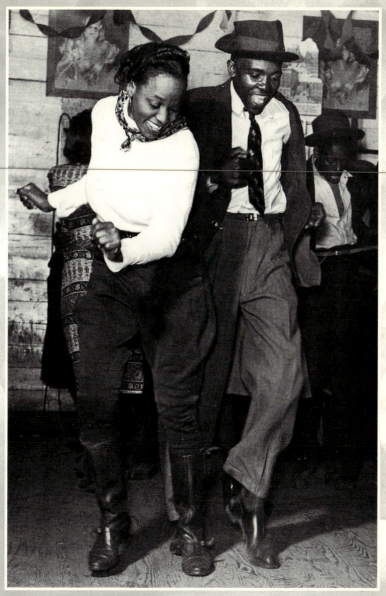

JITTERBUGGING DANCERS in 1939 enjoy a bit of "orderly wicked-
ness" in a Mississippi juke joint, as the rural dance halls are still known.
*(Marion Post Wolcott/Farm Security Administration–Office of War Information
Photograph Collection/Courtesy of the Library of Congress)*

THE TWIST was the last international dance sensation before disco, and Chubby Checker's name was synonymous with the music.
(Ralph Crane/TimePix)

HARRY WAYNE CASEY and bandmate Richard Finch of K.C. & the Sunshine Band helped spark the disco craze by writing the 1974 number one hit "Rock Your Baby" for the then unknown George McCrae. Casey and McCrae are seen here circa 1976. *(Courtesy of Harry Wayne Casey)*

RÉGINE ZYLBERBERG peers out of the peephole of her discotheque in Paris, making sure only the "right" people are admitted—just as Studio 54 would do nearly two decades later. *(Loomis Dean/TimePix)*

SYLVESTER helped bring what was known as "the gay sound"—as early disco was often described—to straight dancers, becoming one of the first openly gay artists to enjoy mainstream success. *(Courtesy of Fantasy, Inc.)*

After being crowned "queen of the discos" by New York deejays in 1975, **GLORIA GAYNOR** went on to become a disco legend with her number one hit "I Will Survive." *(Courtesy of J.P.I.)*

THE SEXUAL ENERGY and the latest in audio, video, and lighting technology of the early gay discos like this one in San Francisco gave disco the edge that later clubs and clubgoers alike were after. *(©Rink Foto SF 1979)*

Her string of number one hits, electric music, and erotic edge made **DONNA SUMMER** the hottest hot stuff in the disco years. In this never-before-published photograph, Summer is seen performing at Madison Square Garden's Felt Forum circa 1978. *(Bobby Miller)*

Tony Manero (played by **JOHN TRAVOLTA,** seen here with Karen Lynn Gorney) became a hero to millions of young Americans when *Saturday Night Fever* and its phenomenally successful soundtrack made disco, almost overnight, an era-defining fad. *(Martha Swope/TimePix)*

After a series of minor rock hits in the sixties, **THE BEE GEES,** shown here at New Year's 2000, became the hottest group in the world in the late seventies by doing for disco what Elvis Presley had done for rock and roll. They put a white face on a distinctly African-American style of music. *(Courtesy of Middle Ear, Inc./Photograph by Bob Soto)*

German music producer **GIORGIO MORODER** introduced the world to the "four-on-the-floor" dance beat—and to Donna Summer—fusing European electronic sound with American R & B and forever changing dance music. *(Courtesy of Giorgio Moroder)*

STUDIO 54 owner Steve Rubell is caught on film by club photographer Bobby Miller one festive night at the famous club. *(Bobby Miller)*

Known as much for showing up naked at Studio 54 as for her striking Afro-Caribbean looks and music, **GRACE JONES** was "fabulousness itself," as *The Advocate* put it. *(Bobby Miller)*

"I know everybody," said Studio 54's resident hostess **CARMEN D'ALESSIO.** "The beautiful, the rich, they are all my friends." Many of those on her eight-thousand-name list could be found dancing the night away at Studio, night after night. *(Bobby Miller)*

One of disco's unique qualities was its ability to bring together young and old, black and white, straight and gay—as illustrated by this **BOOGYING SENIOR** at Studio 54. *(Bobby Miller)*

Club logo for **PARADISE GARAGE**, the legendary New York club where deejay Larry Levan in the early 1980s drove dancers to a frenzy and introduced many to the "speeded-up disco" called house music. *(Courtesy of Mel Cheren)*

The mother of today's out and outrageous drag queens, John Waters's film star **DIVINE** was a Studio 54 regular from the time the club opened, unwinding there after her performances in such late seventies New York classics as *The Neon Woman. (Bobby Miller)*

Was it their sex appeal or the don't ask, don't tell policy of fans that made the **VILLAGE PEOPLE** so famous—and infamous?
(Courtesy of Felipe Rose/William Morris Agency)

An international phenomenon in her own right, **MADONNA'S** string of dance-pop hits and sexually liberated image have made her the most successful dance music artist of all time. She was at her innovative best, fusing vocals and techno sound, in *Ray of Light* (1997) and *Music* (2000). *(Frank Micelotta/Courtesy of Warner Bros. Records)*

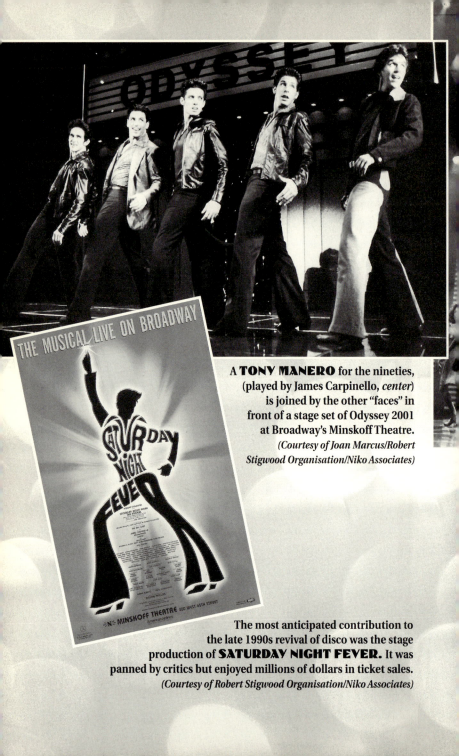

A **TONY MANERO** for the nineties, (played by James Carpinello, *center*) is joined by the other "faces" in front of a stage set of Odyssey 2001 at Broadway's Minskoff Theatre. *(Courtesy of Joan Marcus/Robert Stigwood Organisation/Niko Associates)*

The most anticipated contribution to the late 1990s revival of disco was the stage production of **SATURDAY NIGHT FEVER.** It was panned by critics but enjoyed millions of dollars in ticket sales. *(Courtesy of Robert Stigwood Organisation/Niko Associates)*

Whether in halters and flares or micro-minis and stiletto heels, "the girls" in *Saturday Night Fever* on Broadway prove that **SEXINESS AND SWAGGER** don't belong only to the boys—either in the seventies or today. *(Courtesy of Joan Marcus/ Robert Stigwood Organisation/ Niko Associates)*

Each summer afternoon, **THE BOATSLIP** becomes party central in Provincetown, Massachusetts, keeping thousands of mostly gay revelers grooving to—and purchasing—diva-driven dance music. *(Courtesy of the Boatslip Beach Club)*

Riding high on the wave of disco nostalgia with her 1999 megaselling, Grammy-winning "Believe," **CHER** at age fifty-three showed us the power of disco and dance music to bring people together in the name of fun.

(Barry King/Courtesy of Warner Bros. Records)

where "every night was special and the standards of music, lighting, and partying were constantly being elevated to new heights." The club's deejay, Bobby Viteretti, and light man, Billy Langenheim, were well known among gay discogoers in the late seventies. Crowds roared their approval as the music and lights and their own collective energy raised the temperature ever higher. A large cluster of a dozen mirror balls hanging over the center of the dance floor, the club's signature feature, was accented by an arc light operated from the floor.

In New York, there was Paradise Garage, a gay disco created in the late seventies out of a concrete parking garage on King Street, at the southern edge of the West Village, where new disco records were frequently "auditioned." Only members and their guests were allowed to ascend the steep ramp (the building had been a parking garage) to the dance floor. At Paradise Garage, black, Latin, and gay—the lines among the categories frequently blurred—moved to the beat of superstar deejay Larry Levan's dance mix. From Loleatta Holloway to early house and techno styles, Levan kept New York's wildest dancers moving all night and into the mid-1980s.

The energy of New York and the exclusivity of its most "in" clubs were replicated in nightspots throughout the country. In Chicago, *Time* described Zorine's as "an Art Deco phantasmagoria of mirrors, sweeping staircases, balconies and nooks, in a style evocative of old French Line ships." Despite the $350 membership fee, the club claimed to have twenty-four hundred cardholders. Houston's Élan claimed six thousand members. Even more popular in Houston was Pistachio's, boasting sixteen computer-controlled projectors that splayed images of things like seventies goddess Farrah Fawcett-Majors, diamonds, fire, and snow onto the dance floor.

In Philadelphia, one of the centers of disco music, large arenas were the disco venues of choice. Forty-two thousand people turned out at Veterans Stadium in the summer of 1978 to watch twenty dancing couples compete for a five-hundred-dollar prize. Believed to be the largest audience ever for a disco show, the contest preceded a baseball game by the Philadelphia Phillies. Besides free tickets to the game, runners-up received a T-shirt and the original soundtrack recording for the just-released disco movie *Thank God It's Friday*, starring Donna Summer and the Commodores.

By now discos weren't found only in big cities but in small cities and even smaller towns, too. In Lebanon, Pennsylvania—a town best known for its quality cold cuts—*Billboard* reported that a run of *Saturday Night Fever* in the spring of 1978 had stirred up an "epidemic of disco agitation" among the town's teenagers and young adults. Stoking the disco inferno were several mobile-disco operators who had, as *Billboard* put it, "converged on the county to take advantage of the need for the environment to satiate disco fever." On Friday nights, Stan Horst, the former deejay at Sho-Bar, the town's first disco, had a loyal following among the teens who came to the Annville Union Hose Fire Co. On Sunday nights the disco party moved to the Lebanon Catholic High School auditorium. Adults were also turning out in number for Horst's Friday night disco parties at the Treadway Inn on Route 72 leading into the city. When 528 people showed up for the first one, the disco was moved from the inn's lounge to its larger ballroom.

In tiny Henryetta, Oklahoma, beer was bought at the gas station and slot machines were played at the VFW Hall. But it was against the law to have a public dance. With disco fever panting at its portals, the town held a referendum in August

1978, which upheld the 1957 no-dancing ordinance. Naturally, explained city manager Chester Simons, school dances, VFW dances, and American Legion dances were fine.

On September 16, 1978, more than seven hundred people challenged the Henryetta anti-dancing law by going to the opening night of Crystal Images, a disco in the town's old JC Penney building on Main Street. By 7:30 P.M., seventy-two-year-old Mary Davis and fifty-nine-year-old Ella Paneter were shaking their booties to "Disco Inferno." By closing time, reported *Rolling Stone*, "most of the crowd that had paid the twenty-five-cent cover charge, and many of the eight hundred people lining the street outside, were on their feet and dancing." Police circulated through the crowd snapping pictures of the boogieing scofflaws. Crystal Images owner Gary Moores was charged with operating a dance hall within three hundred feet of an establishment where liquor is served. And about twenty-five people were arrested for disorderly conduct and public intoxication.

Americans were serious about their fun, and disco was seriously fun stuff. In the name of fun and good times, they were even willing to laugh along with a group as outrageous—and outrageously gay—as the Village People. In January 1978, the Southern California Disco DJ Association had named the Village People disco group of the year, and the group was enjoying the rush of its new popularity and record sales. That summer, the group took the country by storm with their second album, *Macho Man.* Besides the title cut, the album showed the group's gay roots in songs like "I Am What I Am" and "Sodom & Gomorrah." In a profile of the band, *Rolling Stone* called the single "Macho Man" "the year's least likely—and funniest—hit single," and said the LP "seems certain to become the first out-and-out disco album without John Travolta on its cover ever to be certified platinum."

Like so many disco acts, the Village People started out as a studio band. The cover of their first album, *Village People*, featured male models wearing mustaches and campy macho outfits. It became an instant disco hit. Their early songs, such as the gay-themed "San Francisco" and "Fire Island," evidenced the effort of French disco producer Jacques Morali and his business partner, Henry Belolo, to appeal to gay clubgoers. Success meant that record label Casablanca wanted a live band to do appearances, so Morali put together the cast of singers and actors who became the Village People: Felipe Rose, the Indian (who actually was part Native American); Randy Jones, the cowboy; Glenn Hughes, the leatherish biker; Alex Briley, the military man; David Hodo, the construction worker; and lead singer Victor Willis, the cop. The new group's first album in 1978, *Macho Man*, became a crossover hit, selling a million copies in the U.S. and millions more worldwide. Six months later, the group released *Cruisin'*, featuring the single "Y.M.C.A."

Their 1978 winning streak continued with *Go West*, featuring the title track and the number-three hit "In the Navy." That year the group performed on top of a float in the annual Macy's Thanksgiving Day parade, reflecting their crossover appeal in the mainstream. How did the Village People account for their mainstream success? Jacques Morali said, "I don't think that the straight audiences know that they are a gay group." The band members, except for lead singer Victor Willis, were gay. Yet they managed to appeal to much of the non-gay American public. Glenn Hughes, the group's biker decked in black leather and chains, explained. "A lot of straight people," he said, "get off on the Americana, the male imagery, and everything else goes totally over their heads. The girls are there because, well, we're six humpy guys and they get off on the sex we're selling. . . . We make ourselves available for as many interpretations as possible."

But it wasn't necessarily the sexual appeal of the Village People that made the band such a big Top 40 success and turned them into symbols of disco's best (fun, danceable music) and worst (pushing a good thing too far). Not only were their songs catchy, but, as Kep Emerson noted in his *Rolling Stone* profile of the band, in their live shows, "so much happens so quickly and the kick-drum pounds so relentlessly that the show becomes a loud blur of hilarity, too patently absurd to be erotic." He added, "You can't help but dance, you can't help but laugh."

There it was, the secret of the Village People's success—and the appeal of disco itself: Make people laugh, help them to loosen up and get down, and they will buy your records, come to your shows, and maybe even dress up to look like you, as fans often did at Village People performances. Spread that playfulness throughout the popular culture, and the result was what *Life* magazine proclaimed in its November 1978 cover story, "DISCO! Hottest Trend in Entertainment," by disco maven Albert Goldman.

SHAKE YOUR GROOVE THING

As 1978 gave way to another new year, millions were doing what *Newsweek* dubbed "The Travolta Hustle." Not only were they dressing like *Saturday Night Fever*'s Tony Manero and his dance partner, played by Karen Lynn Gorney, but they were sporting the star's suave attitude as well. "For many," *Newsweek* noted, "Travolta as Brooklyn disco king Tony Manero has become this generation's rebel without a cause."

The movie and its leading character resonated with young Americans. Checking out the scene at the Right Track, a disco in Pasadena, California, twenty-one-year-old Rudy Guiterrez spoke for many in his observations about *Saturday Night Fever.* "That movie really talked to me," he said. "It told the truth about boring jobs and what the clubs mean to us." His twenty-one-year-old friend Bob Esparaza added, "Here we are somebody. It's how you look and move and who you're with, not the bucks you have."

By carrying yourself just so, and moving on the dance floor as if you were born there, you could be a star in the disco world. For many, the lights, decor, music, and more than anything the collective energy of the crowd itself on a given night, did more than cloak insecurities and hang-ups. The fruits of technology as experienced in the discos—the lights, the new and improved sound systems, the latest designer drugs that were so pervasive in the scene—offered to many something they deeply desired: a sense of freedom and belonging.

At the center of every disco that ever called itself a disco was the singular and unifying symbol of the music, the clubs, and the culture of the seventies—the mirror ball. Covered with hundreds of tiny reflective mirror fragments, high above the crowd, the mirror ball shatters the spots and lasers shined on it into multicolored rays of light, sprinkling them over the pulsing crowd below. Like sparkling champagne bubbles, the colored gems of light heightened the intoxicating effect of the music and the scene—then burst and vanished in the enveloping darkness.

Central as the mirror ball was in the 1970s disco, it had

been associated with dance music and dance spaces since at least the Jazz Age, well before the earliest discotheques. When dancing was sped up in the 1920s—think of the Charleston—the mirror ball was there in the speakeasies, captured in images from the Prohibition era. Huge plaster balls covered with thousands of mirrors, rotated by an overhead motor, fit in perfectly with the glittery flash of the deco period. After World War II, dance palaces with names like the Starlight Ballroom, the Rainbow Room, and Moonlight Pavilion featured mirror balls. In the 1950s, they were suspended above roller rinks and in dance halls. Many a 1960s hallucination was made trippier with the visual thrill of the mirror ball. Finally, in the seventies, when dance music intertwined with popular culture, the mirror ball became the supreme symbol of the flash, glamour, and fleeting brilliance of the disco era.

Beneath the mirror balls, covered in the electric glitter, clubgoers danced the night away to the insistent rhythm of the disco sound. The discos provided an ideal outlet for the primal and driving urge to dance, the music fanning the flames of the disco inferno that had consumed the nation. In their 1978 *Official Guide to Disco Dance Steps,* Jack Villari and Kathleen Sims Villari noted that the new dance trends of the seventies and the packaged, programmed settings for their expression were in many ways simply latter-day examples of the tribal dance rituals practiced by our cave-dwelling ancestors. "As in today's disco," they pointed out, "these primitive dancers usually created a total atmosphere of involvement, using dramatic bursts of smoke and fire, body paint, elaborate costumes, and compelling rhythmic sounds to stimulate all the senses of the participants."

However you danced, the main thing was *that* you danced,

because disco was foremost about dancing and participation. "In fact," said the Villaris, "the disco fever can alter your entire lifestyle, bringing new excitement into your life and giving you a new outlook on your surroundings." That new outlook was precisely what those drawn to the club scene wanted. "So why wait?" asked the dancing duo. "Warm up, tune in . . . and step out!"

As early as 1976, a year before the appearance of both *Saturday Night Fever* and Studio 54, many were already stepping out on the disco scene. And the hustle was *the* dance associated with disco in its early years in the mainstream. Van McCoy's 1975 song "The Hustle" introduced synchronized dancing to the disco scene. The song came about after McCoy's business partner, Charles Kipps, Jr., reported on the Latin hustle he'd seen done at the Adam's Apple, a New York club. McCoy said, "What do you think about a song called 'The Hustle'?" And a Grammy winner and new-old dance were born.

Pablo Yoruba, of Fania Records, told *Newsweek* in 1976, "The hustle is just a bastardization of the mambo. The Latin brothers and sisters heard the black Philadelphia Sound and realized it has the same basic rhythm as salsa. So they took some of the Latin stuff and added their own steps. Out came the hustle." Tito Puente, the famous Latin bandleader, said, "Every new kind of music needs a dance to keep it alive. With disco, it's the hustle." The last musical style to have a dance associated with it, as the hustle was with disco, was the twist. Like the twist, the hustle (and disco music) brought the nation to its feet. As Kitty Hanson put it, "With 'The Hustle,' McCoy did for the seventies what Chubby Checker had done for the sixties—set off a wave that swept people out of their seats and on to their dancing feet."

Not everyone saw the hustle as "the" disco dance. Albert Goldman, for one, disputed the notion that the hustle alone was as important a driving force in the success of disco as some portrayed it to be. "The hustle wasn't any big deal," he said, "just a revival of the traditional Latin dance rhetoric with a couple of 'new' gimmicks, like the Lindy twirl." He noted, however, that the dance's portrayal in *Saturday Night Fever* had gotten at least one thing right. "The one hip thing about the movie treatment," said Goldman, "was that it connected the big nights in the local disco with afternoons at the local studio"—especially in New York, heart and soul of the disco movement. "For years," said Goldman, "thousands of people in New York who wanted to be dancers or maybe just wanted to come on like dancers had been going to these places and working out under the eyes of some very good professional teachers."

When it caught on, disco dancing—the hustle in particular—kept dance schools alive after they had practically faded out of existence in the anything-goes sixties. One New York–based dance school was actually called the New York Hustle, Inc. Its owners, Jeff and Jack Shelly, had started promoting disco dances, including the hustle, as early as 1973. They were happy with their decision, explaining that "being involved with disco dancing from its earliest stages has paid off for us." Among their disco-related ventures were no less than three direct-mail "Learn to Hustle" albums for Columbia House, CBS's mail-order division. John Saionz, owner of a Fred Astaire Dance School franchise in New York, likewise said, "Disco is the best thing to happen to our business in a long time. It has done for dance what the Beatles did for pop music, and it will be around for a long time."

There were other popular disco dances besides the hustle.

One was the bus stop, sometimes called the California hustle, which was a line dance made for group participation. One of the earliest dances created in the discos was the bump. The bump left no doubt about disco's sexual overtones as dancers moved up and down to the rhythm of the music, bumping various body parts against their partners—arms, elbows, knees, hips, and of course the most bumpable of all, the booty. The silliest disco dance step was the disco chicken, often done to Walter Murphy and the Big Apple Band's "A Fifth of Beethoven." Hooking your thumbs under your armpits and flapping your "wings" up and down, you stood on your toes while swinging your knees together. Fortunately, the dance did not call for clucking or pecking.

Still another novelty dance that has, amazingly, become a standard feature of baseball stadiums, weddings, and bar mitzvahs everywhere was the Y.M.C.A., performed to the tune of the Village People's 1979 number-two hit song "Y.M.C.A." Little is required beyond using your hands and arms to spell the word as each letter is sung. For "Y," stand up straight, feet together, and hold your arms above your head and angled in a V shape. For "M," cock your elbows out to the side and angled toward the ceiling, with fingertips touching in front of your chest. For "C," bend your body slightly to the left and extend both arms out with a slight crook in them to form the letter. For "A," your head becomes the base of the triangle as you extend your hands overhead with fingertips touching and creating the apex of the "A."

While synchronized dances were certainly popular in the discos, partnered dancing wasn't the only way of getting down. Another style of dance was even more widely enjoyed: freestyle. While the hustle and such were still popular in places like Queens, at Manhattan's trendsetting Studio 54, "freestyle" dance was the rage. Of course being a "star" was the goal of many disco dancers. For them, freestyle dancing was the answer. All it required is that you let the spirit—and the rhythm—move your body. Grace and coordination were still good to have, but in freestyle dancing there were no steps to memorize. As the name implies, freestyle required little beyond feeling the music and letting go. "Don't fight the feeling!" as K.C. and the Sunshine Band urged in their 1976 number-one hit "(Shake, Shake, Shake) Shake Your Booty." To freestyle, Jack and Kathleen Sims Villari advised, "Try to visualize the music's rhythm emanating from your midsection and radiating out to your fingertips and toes, forcing every muscle to join in. Don't worry if you actually begin to sweat when you practice the dances—it just means you've caught the fever."

One symptom of the disco dance "fever" was the exhibitionism to be found any time people got together to dance. In the discos, it seemed normal. The best example was John Travolta's dramatic solo dance in *Saturday Night Fever*—a far more exciting scene than the much-anticipated dance contest twirl with Karen Lynn Gorney. Albert Goldman said the scene demonstrated "how totally fulfilling it is to dance by yourself as opposed to how frustrating and infuriating it is to have to work out something as intimate as the way you dance with some cranky bitch."

With this kind of emphasis on outshining the others in the constellation of disco "stars," it was only natural that disco culture included its own look and fashions. Many discogoers placed a lot of emphasis on dressing up to get down. Status, for them, meant having the right clothes and accessories. For the gay pioneers of disco, the preferred dance wear was Levi's button-fly 501s, a T-shirt or muscle-T, a mustache, and a colored handkerchief in the back pocket which conveyed one's sexual tastes. Arnie Kantrowitz remembers the look among the "disco clones" in Greenwich Village in the late seventies—the masculine, posturing men who inspired producer Jacques Morali to form the Village People. He said, "They usually wore 'shitkickers,' workboots on their feet, sometimes cycle boots or sneakers. They often wore flannel shirts but removed them or wore tank tops for sweaty dancing. In the summer, sometimes they wore short shorts with workboots and thick socks." Besides this "butch" disco look, there were the "discobunnies" who, Kantrowitz says, "dressed with more glitter and a somewhat more 'femme' approach."

For other discomaniacs, there were three essential disco looks: "basic" disco, "jock" or "roller" disco, and "futuristic." For the men, the "basic" look was either a loud three-piece suit or else tight, high-waisted polyester flared slacks, a print polyester shirt open to reveal gold chains, and of course platform shoes. For the women, it was Danskin tops and wrap skirts, elastic-waisted harem pants, or dresses made from shiny synthetic fabrics that flared out when they were twirled on the dance floor. A feathered hairstyle à la seventies icon Farrah Fawcett-Majors completed the look for women (though some men also went for the feathered fringe—think of Andy Gibb). For both men and women, skin-tight designer jeans were de rigueur. In fact, disco culture spawned the very idea of designer jeans. Impractical as they were for dancing, the jeans illustrated the provocative, body-conscious style of dressing that disco inaugurated.

The jock/roller disco look tended to be more functional than outré—"flashy yet flexible," as *Esquire* put it. The typical outfit consisted of a tank top tucked into shiny, high-cut satin gym shorts, and striped over-the-calf tube socks. Comfort and ease of movement were key. Marlo Courtney, co-owner of Metropolis, a roller disco in Manhattan's theater district that opened in April 1979, said that "serious" skaters had a look all their own. "The guys wear things that are functional and allow for free movement," he explained. "Jeans, loose pants, and big shirts that allow for arm movement are the best. Girls wear the kinds of clothes they might wear to the beach. The clothes people wear here are clothes that move with the body. And they are colorful, just like the people."

One colorful person who has always been a fashion iconoclast—and as enduring a recording artist as ever lived—is Cher. When she wanted to do a publicity event for her disco hit "Take Me Home," her record label, Casablanca, called their other colorful clients the Village People. Felipe Rose, the Indian in the group, recalls, "They called to see if we wanted to roller-skate around the roller rink at Empire with Cher." Not wanting to upstage the star, the Village People left their own costumes at home. Not Cher, though. "Here she is," said Rose, "in these tight spandex pants, a glitter top, and a thing around her head, not quite a rag you tie but like a foam thing. I remember her with the leg warmers around her legs with the skates. And there we were, skating around the rink to 'Take Me Home.' " He called it a "real tacky flashback."

Tacky and flashy defined the "futuristic" disco look. Companies with names like Blink, Blink Jewelry, and Flash in the Pants offered an assortment of jewelry, clothing, and accessories aimed at grabbing attention. Using microscopic circuitry, electrified shirts and jackets sported tiny, blinking lights. White Plains, New York–based Magnamics, Inc., produced a line of suspenders, belts, garters, tote bags, and visors that encased tiny strobe lights. Al Dana's disco shoes, marketed around the country by Arthur Murray Dance Studios and priced at about a hundred dollars, featured clear plastic heels and soles encasing dozens of tiny bulbs that flashed to the beat of the dancer's feet on the disco floor. For the top of the head, Metro-Lite offered fireproof disco wigs in a variety of striking colors; rainbow wigs were especially popular.

For one woman who posted her personal disco tale in cyberspace, the seventies and their fashions were a heyday. "I am forty-two," she says, "and I was the biggest disco freak alive! I wore the nice tight white bell-bottoms with the glittering halter and my favorite eight-and-a-half-inch platforms that were very bright orange. My room was done with red velour and strobe lights and a mini-disco ball. I can't forget about my white shaggin' rug." She adds, "I was a typical *Saturday Night Fever* type of girl."

For "Vincent" and his buds at Brooklyn's 2001 Odyssey—the models for *Saturday Night Fever*'s Tony Manero and crew in Nik Cohn's groundbreaking 1976 *New York* magazine article "Tribal Rites of the New Saturday Night"—being "in" required a dress code as well as certain personal qualities. Those who belonged were called "Faces." They were "a tiny minority," wrote Cohn, "maybe two in every hundred, who knew how to dress and how to move, how to float, how to fly. Sharpness, grace, a certain distinction in every gesture." To qualify for Facehood, they also needed to know how to dance, drive, handle themselves in a fight, use obscenities fluently, be sexually offhanded and tough, and have contempt for everything else but Facehood. As if these more intangible qualities weren't enough, the aspiring Odyssey insider had to be "Italian, between the ages of eighteen and twenty-one, with a minimum stock of six floral shirts, four pairs of tight trousers, two pairs of Gucci-style loafers, two pairs of platforms, either a pendant or a ring, and one item in gold."

At the upper end of the fashion totem pole, disco exerted a major influence on the styles of the late 1970s. The reason was simple: a great many of the leading fashion designers of the time were enthusiastic participants in the disco scene. In New York, center of both the fashion and disco worlds, that meant (at least for a time) Studio 54. Accompanying a larger-than-life photo of John Travolta in the famous white suit he wore in the movie, his arm thrust in the air, a 1998 display outside Manhattan's Fashion Center, illustrating the last century of American fashion, had this to say about the 1970s: "New York's Studio 54 was the center of the fashion universe as disco fever raged and guys in printed body shirts and hipster pants danced the night away with girls in leotards and tie-on skirts, a look that was immortalized in *Saturday Night Fever.*"

For then-rising fashion superstar Calvin Klein, Studio 54 was one of the few places he felt he could find privacy even amid the crowd. He preferred personal comfort to personal fashion statement. Unlike the fashion-conscious wearing his and other designers' creations, Klein and other "new breed" designers were likely to be sporting a casual disco ensemble when they hit the dance floor. At Studio 54, said Klein, "I can dance here at four or five in the morning without people standing around and staring at me, as they do in other places. I can feel at home here whether I'm in a T-shirt and jeans or a sports jacket and pants."

The popularity of Studio 54 among the fashion set ensured that the styles of clothes sported at the disco would make their way to the masses. In 1979, Studio 54 co-owner Steve Rubell said to *Esquire*, "We encourage people to come here who dress like characters, and who make their own clothes. They interest us because they sometimes inspire fashion people to do the next thing. The clothes they choose to dance in here can show up in a designer's collection next year." Rubell noted that one woman who had frequented Studio the year before had always worn velvet. "This year velvet is all over the collections," he said. "I see the association." Capitalizing on its own exclusivity and the sudden interest in designer jeans, Studio 54 launched—and quickly dropped—a line of its own designer jeans, for men and women, featuring the 54 logo stitched on the back pockets. "Now everybody can get into Studio 54," read the ad campaign posters.

Disco-inspired fashion was estimated to account for as much as half of the six billion dollars being spent annually on the disco "industry" at the end of the seventies. Hundreds of boutiques and major department stores across the country did a thriving business in disco accessories. Some stores, Bloomingdale's and Macy's among them, had special departments just for disco accessories, including mirrored sunglasses, sequined suspenders, and hand fans.

For some on the disco scene, standing out meant looking like a walking mirror ball. Nothing wearable said "disco" more than clothing and accessories that were shiny, reflective, and very likely sequined. Whether it was John Travolta's dazzling white suit or the silver body paint of the Tin Man and Tin Woman who turned heads at the opening party of the New York disco Xenon, the object was the same: to throw shade and starlight all at once.

The result was out-and-out camp. Outrageousness was

encouraged. In *Disco Fever,* her 1978 manual on all things disco, Kitty Hanson offered what she considered "legitimate guidelines" (as opposed to rigid rules) for disco dressing. Hanson advised, "Carry a prop. In touch dancing, your hands are engaged with your partner. But free-style disco dancing leaves your hands free. Carry a fan for a sultry Carmen Miranda touch. Wear sunglasses to set you off. Carry big squares of fabric to swirl around as you spin. Wear a muffler—or carry a tambourine. Even your hair can give you something to play with while you are dancing. The main point is, have fun with your accessories."

No fashions were campier or more outrageous, or better captured the essence of the commercial disco scene, than those of Italian fashion designer Elio Fiorucci. By 1979, more than four hundred boutiques around the world bore his name. With prices ranging from moderate to expensive, and ensembles for men and women, Fiorucci fashions included slacks, shirts, skirts and blouses, shoes and sandals, gloves, glasses, handbags that doubled as hats, and every imaginable accessory. Anthony Haden-Guest described Fiorucci as "the fashion store that was mainlining disco, and later punk, into the culture at large."

For those really on the edge, and with lots of money to spend, there was Burghards, an Upper East Side store that served "a disco clientele." Its specialty was the fantasy styles then popular in Berlin. "In Berlin," according to shop clerk Volker, known to regular clients as Vulgar, "the clubs are fashion clubs." He explained, "The patrons must be dressed very freaky, not just your jeans. They won't be allowed in unless they have the look." The look at the time included soft calf shoes tipped with razor-sharp steel points, heavy leather gear studded with nailheads and rhinestones, thigh-high vinyl boots, and gold dancing pumps with five-inch stiletto heels. "The look you need is very whorey," Volker told a woman reporter for *Harper's*. He suggested a pair of black-patent pumps whose ankle straps were actually studded penis rings, adding helpfully, "A girl might wear these with a tigress jacket or a tight sheath of gold Spandex, and her boyfriend could be a motorcyclist."

For many disco fans, the club scene was all about fantasy. Exaggerated, even bizarre, clothing and accessories provided those who needed it with an alternative personality. Whether to let them be open to their sexual fantasies, or simply to attract attention, disco fashions did what all masks do: hide what we want hidden, reveal and even exaggerate what we'd like others to think about us. Other parts of disco culture catered to another rule of human society and the capitalist marketplace, the law of supply and demand. In the case of the movie industry, the supply quickly exceeded the public's demand. The critics' reactions to the movies reflected the arc of disco's rise and fall. But even fans could only stand so much.

MORE, MORE, MORE

Hot after the millions generated by *Saturday Night Fever*, Hollywood did its part to fuel the disco inferno, pumping out disco to the world in the form of disco-themed movies. Before music videos became a standard accompaniment to newly released dance songs, disco movies offered a more multi-dimensional experience of disco than records alone could. A movie offered the look, the music, the lights, the attitude, and the just-folks sorts of characters that people could relate to. The earlier movies featured disco music and clubs as a backdrop to the dramas of daily life. Movie soundtracks were woven into the plots, highlighting and propelling the action.

The first certifiable disco movie was *Car Wash*. The late-summer 1976 semi-musical comedy looks at one day in the life of what *Variety* called "the nuttiest auto laundromat ever seen on the screen." Sully Boyar, the entrepreneur manager of the Dee-Luxe Car Wash, regrets that he didn't go into parking lots like his brother. His nagging wife and Mao-spouting son don't improve his mood. The workers are mostly black, though there are also a Latino, an Indian, and an Anglo—"a lot of likeable street people," as *Variety* put it. The main thing is they are all in it together. Into the crazy mix at Dee-Luxe are stirred customers who get more than the wash and shine they stopped in for. Among them was comedian Richard Pryor as a fancy preacher in a fancy car with a license plate that spells out TITHE and a retinue that includes the Pointer Sisters.

The movie was a big success with a variety of audiences, crossing the lines—as disco music itself did—of black and white, straight and gay. Norman Whitfield's original soundtrack produced some memorable tunes by Rose Royce and the Pointer Sisters, including "Car Wash" and "I Wanna Get Next to You." Noting the music's role in the movie, *Variety* said it was "interpolated so correctly that it might unfairly be overlooked as incidental source music." All in all, *Car Wash* was enjoyed and reviewed as a lighthearted entertainment that used quirky characters and good tunes to look at human foibles and aspirations, and the roadblocks to reaching them. Perhaps because the Dee-Luxe Car Wash was homegrown, the *Los Angeles Times* couldn't say enough good things about the movie. "*Car Wash*," observed reviewer Charles Champlin, "is in fact a very large and special favor—a high-energy, high entertainment, raucously well-observed slice of life."

Popular as it was, though, *Car Wash* reinforced the fact that at the time, disco music, as featured in the movie, was still mainly a big-city phenomenon. It hadn't yet won many converts in Middle America other than lonely teenagers in the heartland aching to get to the Big City. But just over a year after *Car Wash* amused audiences and critics alike, curiosity about "all this fuss over disco" led Middle America to movie theaters to see *Saturday Night Fever*. Essentially a tale about a young man's aspiration to stand out from his blue-collar ethnic crowd, the movie touched a chord in the young and not-so-young alike with its discofied update of the golden American myth that anyone willing to work hard can bring himself up in the world.

The critics were mixed. No one seemed to have anything but a strong opinion about the movie one way or another. In retrospect, some of the critics' negative predictions for the movie show why there is so often a wide gap between the views of critics and the tastes of popular audiences. In the *New York Times*, Janet Maslin said the movie "begins to flag when, after an initial hour filled with high spirits and jubilant music, it settles down to tell its story." She conceded that the music at least "moves with a real spring in its step, and the movie does, too." *Variety* dismissed the movie as "a more shrill, more vulgar, more trifling, more superficial, and more pretentious exploitation film." If that wasn't deadly enough, the reviewer continued, "The clumsy story lurches forward through predictable travail and treacle, separated by phonograph records."

At *New York* magazine, which had published the story that was turned into *Saturday Night Fever*, Molly Haskell tactfully

dismissed the movie. Praising John Travolta as "grace personi-
fied" and an "enormously gifted actor," she nevertheless concluded that "there is nothing an otherwise talented director like
John Badham can do to save the film." What was missing in her
view was "the vital connection, implicit in the story, between
life and the dance, between the hopelessly constricted lives of
the protagonists and the Saturday night ritual."

This wasn't exactly the critical reception the Robert Stigwood
Organization, which produced the movie, expected. But the
film's critical fortunes turned with the help of other critics such
as the *Los Angeles Times*'s Kevin Thomas. In his December 11,
1977, review, Thomas fairly fell over himself with admiration.
"*Saturday Night Fever* is a smash," he wrote, "remaining true to
its source, yet developing it into a full-fledged, thoroughly
absorbing drama, at once poignant and pulsating and infec-
tious as the incessant disco beat that sets its rhythm." Screenwriter Norman Wexler's script was "inspired," gushed Thomas.
John Badham's direction was "luminous." John Travolta delivered a "dazzling performance." Even Ralph D. Bode's cine-
matography was "superb."

Of course, that's the kind of praise that finds its way into
movie advertisements the very next day. It also generates word-
of-mouth interest. It certainly helped to push *Saturday Night
Fever* to become one of the top-grossing films of 1977. And it
surely didn't hurt at Oscar time: in 1978, John Travolta was
nominated for an Academy Award for best actor for his role as
Tony Manero. The movie soundtrack was a big winner in its
own right. Within six months of its release, it had already surpassed any other album in the history of the recording industry. Its success illustrated perfectly what it meant to be in the
right place at the right time. Disco was *it*. Barry Gibb of the Bee

Gees said, "People don't want to hear about how bad times are. I think they are far more interested in dancing and enjoying themselves now. The important thing in life is you're supposed to have a ball."

To Hollywood, the national disco party was a chance to cash in on the fun. Whereas ordinary sharks look at a piece of raw meat and see supper, Hollywood's version of the marine creatures looked at *Saturday Night Fever* through green-tinted glasses and saw a never-ending feast. And not only Hollywood: throughout the world, national film industries produced copycat variations on the theme of the disco dance competition. From Brazil, there was *Vamos Cantar Disco Baby* (1979). Argentina gave the world *La Discoteca del Amor* (1980). In India it was *Qurbani* (1980). A bit behind the curve, Yugoslavia's *Disco* came out in 1984.

Back in the U.S., Tinseltown released another updated fifties teen exploitation flick and at the same time made an important contribution to American slang: *Thank God It's Friday,* or *T.G.I.F.,* as every piece of merchandise associated with the movie was labeled. Hot on the heels of *Saturday Night Fever* in the spring of 1978, *T.G.I.F.* had just about everything going on, all of it happening in the space of a few hours one Friday night at a Los Angeles disco called the Zoo. A young suburban couple try to spice up their marriage by exploring the world of the disco. Two hitchhiking teenage girls sneak in to see the Commodores live and win prize money so they can go to a Kiss concert. Two office girls look for Mr. Right. And Donna Summer, making her film debut as Nicole Sims, crashes the club's live radio broadcast hoping it will rocket her to fame.

Of course, in Hollywood's version of the disco, everyone gets what they come for, and thus it was in *T.G.I.F.* Attempting to prove its blockbuster lineage, ads for the movie said, "Take *Saturday Night Fever,* season it with *American Graffiti,* and you have *Thank God It's Friday."* The critics weren't kind. Vincent Canby was cutting in the *New York Times.* "Miss Summer," he wrote, "whose wigs are as elaborate as Diana Ross's, is competition for the superb Miss Ross in no department other than hair." *Variety* complained, "In this rock revue, players are shoehorned between as many as thirty-two different songs." The magazine at least had faint praise for "Last Dance," Nicole Sims's star turn and Donna Summer's smash hit from the movie, calling it "new and pleasant." Written by Paul Jabara, who appeared as Carl in the movie, "Last Dance" won Summer a Grammy and Jabara an Oscar.

With roller rinks getting into the disco action, it was inevitable there would be movies capitalizing on the popular pastime. The first was *Skatetown U.S.A.* in 1979. Set in a mythical roller disco owned by comedian Flip Wilson, once again everything seems possible. Blond bombshell Greg Bradford is a street skater who has come to the roller disco for (what else?) a contest. Patrick Swayze, in his debut performance, is the black-leather-clad gang member bad guy who of course will do anything to keep Goody Two-shoes from winning. A cast of comic actors provides relief, which makes up most of the movie until the big skate-off. *Variety* called it "a fun, escapist bit of fluff with lots of lights, color, and action but little to think about." Of course, in many ways that could have described what disco itself had become.

Irwin Yablans, producer of the terrifying movie *Halloween,* probably didn't intend to frighten people with his own contribution to the nation's discomania. But *Roller Boogie* is scary if you see it as an example of how low Hollywood will go to turn a profit—and how low the moviegoing public is willing to go right along with it. Starring "chunky little Linda Blair," as the *New York Times*'s Janet Maslin described the *Exorcist* starlet, the movie again worked the skate-contest theme. This time poor-little-rich-girl Blair runs away from home and a brilliant musical career, sleeps in her sports car, and decides that nothing matters more than joining the Venice Beach roller-skating scene. She falls for a geeky roller skater and together they try to save their favorite disco rink from being closed on the eve of a roller-dance contest. Maslin said the movie was "the dopiest movie of the year" in 1979.

By the beginning of the eighties, the disco movies—like the music—became "about" disco itself. And they became really silly. Instead of being about real people's dreams and frustrations and the release the disco could provide, the world of the later movies was limited to the walls of the discotheque. Critics panned their thin-gruel plots and insipid characters. The music itself was increasingly criticized for its monotony. The exasperation of the film critics mirrored the listening public's own growing impatience with paint-by-numbers disco music that had started to sound the same.

Other than producing a few hit songs, the following year's crop of disco-theme movies also revealed the sad truth: disco as a commercial phenomenon, a slot machine that always paid, had just about reached its limit and run out of coins. The evidence was in the movies released in 1980 and the resentful, even savage, responses they elicited among critics.

Showcasing the talents of a group of teenage up-and-comers at Manhattan's High School of Performing Arts, *Fame* was "a lyric poem in praise of freshness, vitality, youth, and talent," according to Charles Champlin of the *Los Angeles Times*.

Others, however, felt the movie's themes were the definition of cliché. With the movie's focus on the angst behind the scenes for the budding young dancers, musicians, and singers, *New York* critic David Denby harrumphed that "show people are climbing on crosses again." Praising all the "attractive young performers," *Time*'s Richard Schickel nevertheless said the movie was a "hokey melodrama" with "a grimy, documentary look to it."

It was a quick tumble downhill from there. Next up to be knocked down in the summer of 1980 was the Village People—sanitized for mass consumption—in *Can't Stop the Music*. The twenty-million-dollar fictional biography of the band revolves around an aspiring disco composer named Jack Morell (the Village People's actual creator was producer Jacques Morali) and a retired model who recruits her friends—a cop, a construction worker, a Puerto Rican Indian, a cowboy, a GI, and a bike-riding leatherman—to form the Village People. David Ansen in *Newsweek* hit the movie and its makers between the eyes. "*Can't Stop the Music*," he wrote, "ushers in a whole new concept in entertainment—it's the first all-singing, all-dancing horror film, the *Dawn of the Dead* of the disco generation." He added, "If this movie doesn't scare you, you're already dead." Even the Village People's hometown newspaper the *Village Voice* called the movie "a certified flop."

In fact, it was a loud and very expensive belly flop. And it wasn't only because *Can't Stop the Music* turned the macho gay Village People into half-baked heterosexuals, robbing the public of the titillation it secretly enjoyed. The times were changing with the new decade, and the welcome for prefabricated disco music and movies had worn thin. Sheila Benson hit it head-on in the *L.A. Times*. "*Can't Stop the Music*," she wrote, "still marches to the music of a disco drummer even while in the suburbs of America the kids are buying buttons that snarl, 'I'd Rather Eat Barbed Wire Than Listen to Disco' and Middle America is embracing bluegrass."

By the time *Xanadu* came out at the end of the summer of 1980, the critics were already smelling the decay of a concept and were more than glad to heave one more celluloid corpse onto the dung heap. Olivia Newton-John, famous for her role opposite John Travolta in *Grease,* portrayed Kira in this twenty-million-dollar "blitz of glitz," as Joseph Gelmis described it in *Newsday.* A kind of tribute to 1940s-style Hollywood musical extravaganzas, the movie also starred a veteran of that era, sixty-eight-year-old dance legend Gene Kelly, as jazz impresario Danny McGuire.

Kira, it turns out, is actually Terpsichore, the ancient Greek muse of dance. The movie was a sort of update of Rita Hayworth's portrayal of the daughter of Zeus incarnated as a Broadway chorine in the 1947 movie *Down to Earth.* Kira is the beautiful girl on roller skates of Sonny Malone's dreams. After Sonny (Michael Beck) falls in love with her, Kira persuades him to join his ex-bandleader friend McGuire—who thinks Kira looks an awful lot like the lead singer in his old band in the forties—in opening a huge roller disco. Having used him to fulfill her mission of establishing Xanadu, Kira reveals her muse status to Sonny, tells him that as a muse she can't feel human emotion, and now that the roller disco is open she must return to the Empyrean.

"So outrageous it's probably critic-proof," observed Gelmis in *Newsday,* "*Xanadu* may well be the gaudiest movie of 1980." *New York*'s David Denby put it a little differently. "Going to see *Xanadu*," he said, "is a little like attending a ball game at the end of the season between two clubs fighting to stay out of last place." Of the perky Newton-John cum Kira, he added, "It's as if Tinker Bell had mutated into the Whore of Disneyland."

Unfortunately, more and more people were feeling by now that disco itself had mutated from something magical into something not unlike a whore as it tried to please everyone. The formula had worn thin and the national disco fever was starting to break.

DON'T STOP 'TIL YOU GET ENOUGH

It seemed for a while that the disco explosion of 1978 would reverberate forever. Percolating beneath the glittery surface, though, was a growing discontent, even anger, with what disco music had become and with the values represented in the disco scene. In late 1978, Albert Goldman's book *Disco* celebrated disco music and culture as perfectly suited to the 1970s sensibility. But by early 1979, even Goldman was changing his mind. "Disco's not art," he said. "It's like a cartoon—it's just a consumer product."

Anti-disco sentiment was nothing new. Despite its huge popularity, not everyone had climbed aboard the disco bandwagon. Some of them, of course, didn't have the physical or mental stamina to ride it. Others abhorred the free-and-easy sexuality and drug use associated with the scene. Still others couldn't get past the early associations of disco with gay men, blacks, and the kind of people they perceived as threats to their idea of the American way of life.

Within the disco world itself, there were rumblings even at the peak of disco's popularity. At Studio 54, the oversold and technically flawed 1977 New Year's Eve bash had set the pace for the year that followed. Co-owners Steve Rubell and Ian

Schrager were beset with lawsuits by angry patrons who had been roughed up by bouncers as they tried to get into the club. And their slippery accounting practices attracted the attention of the IRS.

Just as *Newsweek* was proclaiming disco's takeover, the ultrahip were proclaiming the end of Studio 54. In April 1979, almost two years to the day after the disco opened, *Esquire* nightlife columnist Taki Theodoracopulos wrote that "the truly in crowd, those people who do not rely on P.R. men to place their names in tomorrow's gossip columns, has been staying away from the place as if it were Cambodia." Although New Yorkers were "known as the most masochistic people on earth" for their willingness to be treated badly for the sake of being "in," Taki (as he calls himself) said Studio 54 patrons "were insulted, pushed, and beaten up once too often."

With more of Studio 54's core crowd going to other discos, such as the just-opened Xenon, Taki said Studio 54 would be left to the "slobs." Just who might they be? As Taki so vividly put it, "the bisexuals from the suburbs, the would-be beautiful people, the Biancas from the Bronx, the shameless celebrity spotters, and all the other twitchy-nosed nocturnal lowlifes who lay fruitless siege to the doors of Studio 54." Now even the non-pedigreed could get in—which was fine with the self-anointed trendsetters. They hardly wanted to be seen among what Taki called "the freaks, transvestites, groupies, and professional gays who at present are masquerading as the in crowd at Steve Rubell's version of capitalist decadence."

By the end of 1979, not only was Studio 54 suffering from the competition, but the world's most famous disco was imploding because Rubell and Schrager had skimmed $2.5 million from the club's revenues without paying taxes—and they got caught. In a November 1979 cover story in *New York*, "Studio 54: The Party's Over," Henry Post said that not even the club's fifteen lawyers—including Studio 54 regular Roy Cohn, the infamous attorney who assisted Senator Joseph McCarthy's witch-hunt for Communists in the 1950s—could save Rubell and Schrager. They had filed a 1977 tax return claiming a net taxable income of only forty-seven thousand dollars during the club's first year of operation. But garrulous Rubell had let slip to at least one friend that the club actually took in upwards of four million dollars for the year. In fact, in 1977 Rubell had bragged to *New York*, "The profits are astronomical. Only the Mafia does better."

Using a double set of books, Studio 54's owners tried to avoid tax-evasion charges. They claimed that to pay bills they had put hundreds of thousands of dollars in a black plastic garbage bag in the ceiling panels of the basement. But the U.S. Attorney's office found the actual split records for 1977, as well as a safe-deposit box with nine hundred thousand dollars in cash at a Citibank branch. U.S. District Judge Richard Owen sentenced Rubell and Schrager to three and a half years in prison. As it turned out, they spent only a year behind bars before their release to a halfway house, where the former night owls had an eleven o'clock curfew.

After their release, the once-popular duo were ostracized by many of their good-time friends. Studio 54 regular Andy Warhol, who had formerly referred in his diaries to Rubell as "Stevie," now called him "Stephen." In *The Last Party*, his own memoir of Studio 54, Anthony Haden-Guest quotes the writer Dotson Rader as saying, "Nobody wanted to know Rubell when he got out of jail." Rader recounted an awkward scene that illustrated how far the formerly high and mighty had fallen. As he and his friends Tennessee Williams and the famed director of Eugene O'Neill's plays Jose Quintero sipped cocktails at the Pier House Hotel in Key West, Florida, Rader spotted Rubell standing at the bar looking "terrible." He said, "Look, Tennessee! It's Steve Rubell." Williams said nothing.

After chatting with Rader at the bar, the disgraced club owner came over to the table where the group was sitting. Rader invited him to have a seat. "Baby, that seat is taken," said Williams to Rader, ignoring Rubell. "It is not!" protested Rader. "That seat is *occupied*!" said Williams, closing the conversation. After Rubell drifted away, Rader proposed inviting him for dinner. Williams simply said, "I don't want to sit down with a *jailbird*."

The shunning of Rubell and Schrager was happening in a different way within the disco business itself. Many of those professionally affiliated with the music also began to regret their association with what disco had become. The rich early sounds of American R & B and soul artists, fused in the mid-seventies with imported Euro-disco electronics, had given way to music whose most obvious quality was repetition. "It all sounds alike," was a common complaint. As soon as disco music caught on with the mainstream, it began spawning what *Billboard*'s Radcliffe Joe described as "armies of speculators intent on piggybacking on the successes of those true innovators who had blazed the trails which helped establish the credibility of the concept." The success of *Saturday Night Fever*'s soundtrack wrongly convinced the recording business that people would buy anything with a disco beat.

The mass-produced sound of late-1970s disco wasn't entirely welcome in the gay club scene, where disco music had found its first toehold in the popular culture. Adam Block, the rock critic for the national gay and lesbian newsmagazine *The Advocate* from 1976 to 1996, says it was the "enforced, predictable conformity" of disco that bothered him. "My problem with disco was monotony," he said, "the ghettoization and conformity . . . replacing provocation and possibility with, say, the Village People."

The shortsightedness of radio programmers revealed itself in their ignorance of the fact that because disco music is intimately tied to disco dancing and discotheques, it was, as Radcliffe Joe put it, "difficult, if not impossible, to capture and hold the ambience of the music's natural habitat." By the time 1980 rolled around, the novelty of the disco sound had already worn off for many listeners, and advertisers were disenchanted with the lower-than-hoped-for sales power of the all-disco stations. Besides the limited ambience that disco radio could provide, there were other problems as well. There was the unavoidable repetition of the music. And twelve-inch disco dance records didn't lend themselves to radio's regular breaks for news, traffic, weather reports, and commercials.

Much as New York all-disco station WKTU-FM's rise to the top was hailed as a sign of disco's fabulousness, the fact is that within weeks of the station's pinnacle, it already began to show signs of slippage. By September 1978, only two months after adopting its all-disco format, it slipped from an 11.3 percent market share to 9.2 percent. The format's uncertainty continued to cause jitters at WKTU during the next year that it kept its disco playlist. Finally, in December 1979, the station adopted another, decidedly non-rock format, playing the mellow music of vintage artists such as Glenn Miller, Frank Sinatra, and Tony Bennett. The word "disco" was virtually banned at the station.

Disco artists themselves were often caught between the

popularity and affluence they enjoyed because of disco and their self-respect as musicians. Melba Moore, a Broadway singer turned disco diva who hit it big with "You Stepped into My Life," said, "We're in a period of the McDonald's of music, where it's mass-marketed like junk food." She added, "I don't know what *good* is anymore."

Among nightclubs, there was an attempt by those who were making big bucks off the disco concept to steer clear of what they saw as the taint of disco. Even in the hottest summer of disco's biggest year, there were new clubs opening that tried to distance themselves from the stereotypes and even standard features of the disco scene. One club that opened in Denver in the summer of 1978 hoped to attract jet-setters by insisting it be known as a discotheque—not, heaven forbid, a disco. The club, Reflections of Mr. Pippins, prohibited such standard disco wear as blue jeans, T-shirts, halter tops, shorts, tennis shoes, and even men's hats. "We'd like to see people in coats and ties," said manager Norman Rosenstein. Anyone showing up looking high would be asked to leave. To underscore its "seriousness" and emphasize its difference from "what disco was coming to," Rosenstein said that even the music would be different. "It will be leaning toward European disco," he explained, though he couldn't describe what he meant by "European disco."

Like their counterparts in the recording industry, Hollywood moviemakers thought the public would pony up its money for anything made of celluloid featuring a disco motif. But the critics, at least, weren't buying. From the early disco movies in which disco music provided the soundtrack of the lives on the screen, Hollywood's version of disco had devolved into paper-thin characters and even thinner plots focusing on the disco "lifestyle."

The intelligentsia were only too happy to raise their own bleats against the self-perpetuating disco fad in the cerebral journals read by academics and political junkies. Pop-music critic Jim Miller acknowledged in *The New Republic* in 1979 that disco music was "the music of our times." The genre had produced some "great pop music," he conceded. And "the vital pulse of what's happening" had improved the lot of the largely black musicians making it. "For lapsed hippies and jet-setters anxious about aging," said Miller, "it is a comforting way to pretend you can stay young by staying in step with changing fashions." His gripe was with what disco had become in the hands of the capitalists fanning the flames of the disco inferno burning up the country. "The broader disco culture," said Miller, "is also a hustle, a game, a mildly diverting new form of conspicuous consumption."

The criticism within disco's own ranks and among the cultural elite was minor compared to what was brewing in the nation's pockets of red-blooded conservatism. In Oklahoma, J. B. Bennett, an unsuccessful candidate for the state senate, actually staked out an anti-disco platform. He promised to "stand with you on your efforts to stop and eliminate corrupting influences on our young citizens," as one of his advertisements put it.

In Tulsa, the director of a local Y.M.C.A. wrote a letter to city radio stations suggesting they "give some thought" before playing the Village People's big hit "Y.M.C.A." He felt the city's number-one disco song "doesn't give an image that's anything like our Y.M.C.A. or any of the other Y's in Tulsa." He noted that the National Board of Y.M.C.A.s was considering a "trademark infringement" suit against the Village People and their record company, Casablanca. Steve Keator, the label's national publicity and media director, was quoted as saying, "I think the whole matter is totally absurd." He pointed out that a number of Y.M.C.A.s throughout the country had actually thanked Casablanca for the free publicity.

Anti-disco sentiment simmered beneath the surface of the culture, mostly grumbling and occasional snide comments. The narcissism and hedonism of the club culture was abhorred by those who make a career denying their own "isms" and "phobias." The Reverend Billy Sunday's condemnation of the tango in 1915—"the most hellish institution that ever wriggled from the depths of perdition"—echoed down the century in similarly condemnatory words in the late 1970s. Despite the still-tremendous popularity of disco music, perhaps because of it, a campaign against it began to build steam. "Disco sucks, rock lives!" was the rallying cry of the disco-haters. *Newsweek* observed in the summer of 1979, "Most dissenters are rock 'n' roll fans who deplore disco's monotonous rhythm, and some view the fad as an extension of the narcissistic Me Decade."

But with this kind of venom spewed at disco, one had to wonder. What was *really* getting their dander up? Were they merely criticizing the cookie-cutter music? Some of the artists themselves did that. Were they condemning the loose living of the painted lady that disco had become? Many fans of the music did that. Or were they lashing out—perhaps unconsciously, perhaps conveniently in the guise of a musical-taste difference—at the blacks and gay men who had been the driving forces behind disco?

Bernie Lopez, creator of the Web site discomusic.com, had

just started high school when he first realized that some people felt so much bitterness toward disco. He recalls, "I was into art, so I joined the art club. There were older students, now I realize they were gay. They brought in a record called *Salsoul Christmas Jollies*. I had never heard it before, and I thought it was really funny." Others were pretty uptight about it, though, said Lopez. "It wasn't even 'I'd rather listen to Led Zep than Jethro Tull.' It was really mean, vicious."

Mostly the anti-disco mood was harmless. There were T-shirts saying things like STAMP OUT DISCOS IN OUR LIFETIME and even SHOOT THE BEE GEES. But in July 1979, the anti-disco fever turned to actual flames. Chicago radio shock jock Steve Dahl, "a militant anti-disco agitator," as *Newsweek* described him, invited his fans to bring their disco records to "Disco Demolition Night" at the city's Comiskey Park. A crowd of forty-nine thousand mobbed the stadium, home of the Chicago White Sox, a third of them hanging on to their disco discs with child-like anticipation. For the ninety-eight-cent entry fee they were offered the chance to vent their anger against disco during the break in the evening's scheduled double-header.

As it turned out, the second game was never played. When Dahl detonated the records in center field, seven thousand fans rushed onto the playing field. "Before police could chase them back to the stands," reported *Newsweek*, "they had destroyed the batting cage and the pitcher's mound and set several small fires."

If the fires didn't burn Chicago to the ground like the great fire a century before, they did seem to retch out noxious clouds as destructive as the acid-rain clouds caused by the Midwest's smog-spewing factories. It was almost uncanny how quickly disco's popularity with the public began to decline not long after the sordid events in the Midwest. Joyce Bogart, the widow of Casablanca chief Neil Bogart, recalled "the amazing end of it all!" Middle America rose up against the monotony of disco music and the narcissism and hedonism of disco culture. And when the fad ended, it ended as quickly as it began. "It died an incredibly quick death recordwise," said Bogart. "It took us all by surprise."

By the end of 1979, *Rolling Stone* said, "You can say that the first six months [of 1979] belonged to disco . . . and that the last six months belonged to brave young rockers." But in the case of rock versus disco, it wasn't just back-slapping rock versus namby-pamby disco. It was a symbolic matter of who's on top and who's on the bottom—as is so much in human society, from the bed to the boardroom. Peter Braunstein said in the *Village Voice* in 1998 that "the real animosity between rock and disco lay in the position of the straight white male." He explained, "In the rock world, he was the undisputed top, while in disco, he was subject to a radical decentering." Testosterone-driven rock had to reassert its role as alpha male in the pop-music world. And as Braunstein put it, "Only by killing disco could rock affirm its threatened masculinity."

Despite the rockers' resentment, the disco machine cranking out the discs had in actual fact become its own worst enemy. Music lawyer Fred Gershon said that after RSO Records did so well with the *Saturday Night Fever* and *Grease* soundtracks, other record companies were tripping on the anticipated fumes of the greenbacks they too expected to make on disco. As he put it, "The expectations of every record company became totally demented and deluded because they all saw that little RSO Records was able to become a half-billion-dollar-a-year company."

Giorgio Moroder, the legendary German producer who brought the world Donna Summer and Euro-disco electronics, said, "Certainly disco killed itself. And there was a terrible backlash. Too many products, too many people, too many record companies jumping on this kind of music. A lot of bad records came out. I guess it was overkill."

Felipe Rose, the Village People's Indian, calls them "disco murderers," the record companies, the promoters, the television shows that fed the disco fever even after it was breaking. "It got to the point," said Rose, "where it was so hideous and overdone, and there was a backlash afterward and it wasn't fun." Rose failed to mention that many—including many gay disco fans—saw the Village People themselves as symbols of the silly spectacle that disco had become.

What the rockers couldn't do with their own infernos, what the holy rollers couldn't do with their anti-disco soul-saving campaigns, disco did to itself. The disco inferno turned into a giant meltdown. The crassness and mass production were coming to be seen for what they were: efforts to exploit to death what had started out as something very positive, and to keep the wheels of capitalism turning by making even bigger fortunes for the already fortunate. As Felipe Rose puts it, "Once the light stopped and the ball stopped spinning, everyone realized that, shit, it's not as glamorous as we thought."

As the 1980s got under way, disco was virtually a cussword. "Disco had a stigma now," as Bernie Lopez puts it. The record companies tried to keep the fever going, still producing new disco music. But radio stations weren't programming it anymore because the public had grown tired of the 24-7 boogie beat. To placate the now-open hostility to disco, the record companies changed the wording on their record labels from

12-INCH DISCO SINGLE to 12-INCH RELEASE or ADVANCE RELEASE. Instead of "disco," they now called it "dance music." Mike Misulich, a former deejay at Lord Lindsay's, a disco in an old church in Knoxville, Tennessee, recalled that there used to be "racks and racks of disco labels" in the late seventies at the Record Bar in his hometown. "Suddenly," he added, "in what seemed like a week's time, they dwindled to a few with plain white labels."

In the plain-white-label eighties, many looked at the seventies and everything associated with them as best left in the past. Nothing could be "deader than disco," a popular phrase in the straitlaced new decade. As Felipe Rose recalls, "You couldn't even admit to people that you had disco records in your house." Bell-bottoms were silly; straight-legs and button-down shirts were in.

As President Reagan's "Morning in America" dawned, all too many Americans willingly moved with the former actor from the Me Decade into the Greed Decade. Drug use—in public, at any rate—was passé. For gay men, disco's original and strongest supporters, the coming-out party of the seventies gave way to memorial services for the AIDS-stricken in the eighties. Excess was out, abstinence was in.

There was no room in the "just say no" sobriety of the eighties for the escapist zaniness of the seventies. Those who predicted the disco madness would last forever seemed to have inhaled or swallowed a little too much something-or-other a little too often. Tastes and the times had changed. The public's obsession with disco passed almost as quickly as it had appeared. Fickle Americans had already moved on. From disco, the popular-musical taste shifted to country, as that traditional style of American music spoke to the new era now trying to reclaim through its foggy memories the "traditional values" of a time long past.

Shedding the weight of all the fantasies that had been hung around its neck, it was time for disco to go back underground. Disco music—and, especially, the divas who made it—would remain extremely popular in the gay club scene that had nurtured it in the early seventies, before the mainstream "discovered" it. And even if it disappeared as "disco" from the popular mainstream, disco music would continue to spawn new generations of dance music down to the present. The spirit of the boogie lived on, even if in the eighties no one would be caught dead using the word "boogie" and meaning it in any way but ironically.

After the passing of disco as a fad and remarkable pop-cultural phenomenon, what was left was the best part of all: really terrific dance music. Those who still embraced it had known all along that it was music meant to move the feet, not drive an entire popular culture. Evolving into other styles of dance music, yet continuing to thrive largely intact as "club" music among culturally influential subcultures—gays and African-Americans—disco was poised for a resurgence if the time was ever right again. Could it happen? Would we want it to, given all the not-so-good things that disco came to stand for? Or could we take what we liked and leave the rest?

4

WHY IT LIVES ON

Studio 54 co-owner Steve Rubell once said, "A club is about capturing a moment in time." Reflecting on the relatively short thirty-two months of the most famous disco's peak, he added, "Not a very long moment, either." The disco fad was like that, too. It grew out of the right music (upbeat) happening at the right time (when people needed a lift from the troubled times). But then the times, and the public's mood, changed again. It would never be the same as one brilliant light of 1970s nightlife was snuffed out after another. Many discos closed as more people did their dancing in aerobics classes and exchanged their daiquiris for Gatorade. Rubell himself died from hepatitis in 1989. Many other Studio 54 habitués died in the AIDS epidemic of the 1980s and 1990s. "Half the people who used to be there are dead," said Carmen D'Alessio, the club's celebrity recruiter. Bianca Jagger, for whom lavish parties were once thrown at Studio 54, said, "I would rather die than talk about Studio 54. I wish it never existed."

As the 1980s got under way, many felt disco was dead. Some, like Jagger, even regretted their own enjoyment of it. The word "disco" was dropped by radio stations, record labels, and those on the cutting edge of popular-music culture. The commercial oversaturation of disco, and the disco scene's collapse into narcissism and self-destructive behavior, helped kill off the public's obsession with it. The repetitive four-on-the-floor beat became exactly that, repetitive. Yet the club scene lived on, if on a smaller scale, still providing outlets for hearing dance music and dancing. But the music played in the clubs now could be any of a variety of dance-music styles that grew out of disco and its various components.

In the last decade of the last century, as the twenty-year nostalgia cycle came inevitably around and people needed an outlet for their pre-millennial jitters, 1970s disco music and even 1970s fashions became "retro." Being the rhythmic creatures we are, it was inevitable that the need to dance would eventually get the best of us. Because the nineties were a decade when new fads in sensual pleasure—cigar smoking comes to mind—were enjoyed in discriminating moderation, it was natural that those seeking the release and pleasure of dance would want only the best dance music ever made. Naturally, they rediscovered disco.

I WILL SURVIVE

The demand for public dance spaces outlived Studio 54 and the multitude of other nightspots that arose in the late 1970s to cater to and exploit the public's taste for disco. But the most famous disco of them all had raised the bar for dance clubs. Sophisticated light shows, the very best sound systems, top-name deejays, and a terrific mix of dance music were required and standard features of the discos that were no longer called by that name. In New York, laboratory of virtually every trend in American popular culture, two major post-disco discos opened in the early 1980s. The Saint, the most famous of gay discos, opened in September 1980. And in 1984, former Studio 54 co-owners Steve Rubell and Ian Schrager opened the Palladium.

Housed in the old Fillmore East building, the Saint was instantly famous for its tremendous size, its sexually active mazes and balcony, the round dance floor seventy-six feet in diameter, and the forty-foot domed ceiling with its hidden door. Through that door both a giant mirror ball and live performers were lowered above the crowd to provide music from on high. Men who were there fondly recall the time Betty Buckley was lowered from the ceiling to reprise her hit from *Cats,* "Memory." More than anything, the Saint was known for the energy generated by the thousands of dancers bumping and grinding into the wee hours. Its black-and-white theme parties were the hottest tickets in town for many gay men on the dance scene. Years after the club closed, the "Saint-in-Exile" would continue these theme parties in venues around Manhattan. Unfortunately, the club gained a different reputation when AIDS was first reported in 1981 among some of the gay men who frequented it. In fact, one of the earliest names of the plague was "the Saint's disease." When it was good, though, the Saint was extraordinary. Arnie Kantrowitz observed in *The Advocate* that "ecstasy occurs regularly at the Saint." Advertising posters for the club featured Kantrowitz's words.

The Palladium was perhaps the best-known of the second generation of great non-gay discos in New York. Its rectangular dance floor was enclosed by three-story-high illuminated balconies on two sides. Two large robotic arms, each holding banks of twenty-five video monitors, wandered over the dance floor. Like other dance clubs, the Palladium also featured several different specialized clubs-within-the-club in one building, including the neo-psychedelic maze of rooms and lounges in the basement. Steve, the former deejay behind the Web site "5 am ago," says, "The dimensions of the club were mind-blowing; everything was big, stylish, and unprecedented, and you could spend the entire night just wandering through the place—from balcony to basement—and meet an interesting mix of friends, freaks, and better-than-average-basic-club-types."

In other dance clubs of the immediate post-disco years, such as New York's Private Eyes, deejays experimented with remixing music tracks. The result was ever-newer styles of underground dance music, particularly house music. With thirty-four video screens, Private Eyes also popularized video as a new feature of successful dance clubs. Taking a page out of Studio 54's own theatrical playbook, the club's most famous party was for Chic leader Nile Rodgers's first solo LP. In a takeoff on his name, the entire club was decorated with an Egyptian theme, including live camels and ten tons of sand mixed with glitter dumped outside its front door to give a desert-oasis appearance. All of the video screens showed *Cleopatra* and *Lawrence of Arabia*. Describing the party, Stephen Saban wrote in *Details*, "The nice part about Private Eyes is that it doesn't matter, really, who's there—there's always something fascinating being mixed on all those screens. And it's so air-conditioned, you can dress."

The theatrics of the post-disco years were rarely as spectacular as in the no-holds-barred seventies, but the main event at every dance club was still what it had been in the disco years:

the music. Disco had staked out the territory for dance music to become a distinct, legitimate genre. And just as dance-music styles had evolved to form disco in the 1970s, disco music itself would continue to evolve down the years into different dance-music offshoots.

Even after the disco fad faded from the mainstream, great disco songs were still being turned out, if in smaller pressings—and now simply called "dance music" to avoid the stigma (once again) attached to disco. In 1980, Stephanie Mills gave us "Never Knew Love Like This Before." The S.O.S. Band helped us do it right in "Take Your Time." Teena Marie carried on disco's focus on romance with "I Need Your Lovin'." And in the very last certifiable "disco year," 1982, the Weather Girls stormed the barricades of the night with their anthem "It's Raining Men."

Throughout the eighties, the synthesizers and drum machines that were first used by disco producers like Giorgio Moroder became more sophisticated. This allowed music to become more mechanized—"an excursion into a sonic never-land," as the *New York Times*'s Jon Pareles put it. Listening to Donna Summer's 1975 hit "I Feel Love" today is a reminder of what a departure disco music really was from the music that had come before it, particularly in its use of the electronic sounds that originated in Europe. It is also a reminder of how little really changes over time. Great dance music retains its power to give dancers what they want: an altered state where body and soul are one and both are lost in the music, the moment, and the physical exuberance of the dance.

In the early 1980s, after the disco fad had run its course, the black American rhythm and blues that had fused with European electronics in disco music in the late seventies once again defused in cutting-edge styles of dance music. Dance-music styles splintered into four basic subgenres, each of which occasionally borrowed from the others. Growing out of the underground American dance scene, as disco had done, there was house, essentially disco with an even faster rhythm. Extremely popular in Europe, though it originated in the U.S., techno music and its many offshoots grew out of the mechanized styles that first appeared in disco in the mid-seventies. American rhythm and blues moved toward the smooth sound of urban soul and the verbal rhythm of rap, spawning the hip-hop "ghetto" culture. Finally, there was the "dance-pop" style of dance music. Perhaps the purest descendent of disco, this style has had great pop crossover success. It has also been extremely popular in many gay clubs where disco-style dance music continued to be embraced long after the mainstream fad had passed.

The first post-disco dance-music style not to be called "disco" was Hi-NRG. Driven by a fast drum machine and synthesizers, and with only slight hints of pop, it could include disembodied vocals, but it was mainly about the beat. Miquel Brown's single "So Many Men, So Little Time" and its B side, "High Energy" (Record Shack Records, 1989), are excellent examples of Hi-NRG. Hi-NRG gave rise to techno and house music, which went in two different directions—house was the more funk and soul sound, techno the more mechanical.

Another popular dance-music style right after disco was new wave, which combined the energy and irreverence of punk rock with the four-on-the-floor beat of disco, and featured high production values like disco in what was essentially pop music. Unlike traditional rock, new wave featured electronics and synthesized production. Although it became a catchall term, new wave caught on in dance clubs as disco was fading. Groups like Culture Club, the Go-Go's, Eurythmics, the B-52's, and the Human League made songs that were hits with both dancers and radio listeners, just like disco. The Human League's all-synthesizer sound—as in their most famous single, "Don't You Want Me?"—helped usher in the "synthpop" sound of 1980s pop music.

New wave music sparked a minor fad of its own, featuring Alice Cooper–like clothes and demeanors. Young people like Will Moppert in the early eighties sported new wave looks and attitudes—their way, says Moppert, of rebelling against disco while still allowing them to be "bizarre-looking." The rainbow of vivid colors from the disco years was now reduced to cold, hard black. In his early twenties at the time, New Jersey native Moppert said, "I remember all my family laughing at me because my friends were all these whacked-out-looking people with big hair, black eye makeup, and white faces, dressed in black."

House music, which pop-music historian Ed Ward describes as "disco music speeded up," was created by urban deejays, particularly in gay clubs, who altered dance music to make it less pop-oriented. Larry Levan, the well-known deejay at Manhattan's Paradise Garage, was one of house's chief pioneers. In house, the beat became more mechanical, the bass grooves deeper, and elements of synthpop, rap, and jazz could be grafted over the steady discolike four-four beat. The music was often purely instrumental. When there were vocalists, they were the kind of faceless female divas who often made disco music. By the late 1980s, house had broken out of underground clubs in cities like Chicago, New York, and London, and even made incursions into the pop charts through the records of artists like Erasure and Madonna. House got its name from a

Chicago warehouse in which local deejays first spun their "bright-timbered, shuffle-beat, libido-intensive remixes," as Mark Jacobsen described it in *Esquire*. House split into a number of subgenres, including ambient house, progressive house, and acid house. House influences can still be heard in many pop songs today.

While house was still explicitly connected to disco, techno was strictly electronic music. Originating in Detroit, techno grew out of house but did away altogether with anything like a vocal track and, for that matter, anything human-sounding at all. Detroit techno was picked up in Berlin, London, and Antwerp, influential centers for European dance music. At his home in Berlin, Ed Ward explained that Berliners, "coming out of the Kraftwerk tradition," and Belgians, coming out of "new beat" music, produced a distinctive European electronic dance-music style that would become typified by the English group New Order. Although it has had limited appeal in the U.S., techno quickly became—and remains—the most popular style of dance music in much of the rest of the world.

A grab bag of other microgenres of techno music, their differences often barely discernible even to a popular-music expert, rounded out the late 1990s dance scene. They included tribal, jungle, trance, ambient, and the jungle offshoot drum-and-bass that was hugely popular in Europe. To show how far techno has come from its disco ancestor, Ward noted that in European dance music, "disco" is an "ironic" term and, at best, just an ingredient. He added, "Americans seem to need vocals, for some reason."

Vocals remained distinctly important in post-disco American rhythm and blues, particularly in the rap music popular with young black audiences and white suburban teens. The

131 • WHY IT LIVES ON

lyric, an important component of African-American musical styles—often dispensed with or merely sampled in electronic music—remained key in R & B, as did the interplaying rhythm of words and music working together for effect and attitude.

From its beginning, rap often borrowed from disco music's melodies and lyrics. The first rap record, Sugar Hill Gang's "Rapper's Delight" in 1979, used the entire bass line of Chic's "Good Times." Puff Daddy sampled Diana Ross's "I'm Coming Out" in the Notorious B.I.G.'s rap anthem "Mo' Money, Mo' Problems." Rap began as a simple style with vocalists rapping over scratched records and drumbeats. Hard-core rappers, such as Run-D.M.C., kept the beats to a minimum and emphasized the lyrics. The edgy rhymes and sample-heavy beats of Public Enemy were cutting-edge American music in the eighties and nineties.

Hip-hop—a catchall term for the hard-edged culture surrounding rap music—has taken even more freely from disco, to the point of using the entire melodies of disco songs but changing the lyrics. The alternative group Len, for example, made a song called "Don't Steal My Sunshine"—new words over the melody of the Andrea True Connection's "More, More, More." Like other styles, rap spun off a range of subgenres, including East Coast rap, West Coast rap, gangsta rap, Southern rap, pop-rap, trip-hop, and big beat.

Anyone going to a dance club at the end of the last century and beginning of the new millennium could have heard any of these dance-music styles. As in the disco years, club deejays were the real stars—particularly in the underground rave parties where acid house was played and large quantities of drugs, especially ecstasy, were consumed. Unlike disco, though, the newer dance music frequently played on feelings like anger and alienation. Happy, cathartic dancing to fun-spirited music wasn't as important as a head trip, drug induced as often as not. In a mark of just how far mainstream dance music had come since the days of disco's lush sounds and catchy vocals, the *New York Times*'s Jon Pareles noted in 1997, "During the nineties acoustic instruments all but disappeared, and songs have shrunk to catchphrases like 'Wiggle It' [by 2 in a Room, 1990] and one-chord electronic pulses like Sandy B's 1996 'Make the World Go Round.' "

And yet, bubbling right alongside the mechanical mini-malism and shameless sampling was dance-pop, disco's truest musical heir. Like disco, its distinguishing features are lyrics, a simple, catchy melody over a pounding dance-club beat, and a more human (rather than mechanized) quality. Dance-pop has been especially important in the gay dance scene, says Ed Ward, because "gay taste in dance music has been 'diva-centric' " For this reason, he added, "Styles popular in Europe haven't caught on in the U.S." The musical heroes of the 1980s and 1990s gay dance scene included such artists as Jimmy Somerville, Mark Almond, Frankie Goes to Hollywood, Depeche Mode, Erasure, aha, the Pet Shop Boys—and, above all others, Madonna.

Dreaming of becoming a ballet dancer, Madonna Louise Veronica Ciccone, the third of eight children, moved from her native Michigan to New York in 1977, where she studied with choreographer Alvin Ailey and modeled. In 1979, Madonna joined the disco group Patrick Hernandez Revue, singing backup on the hit "Born to Be Alive." Her first single, "Every-body," became a club hit at the end of 1982. "Holiday," from her debut album, *Madonna*, became Madonna's first Top 40 hit in October 1983, followed by the Top 10 "Borderline" in March

1984. Her second album, *Like a Virgin,* was produced by Nile Rodgers and released at the end of 1984.

Cultivating a public image that ranged from the sluttish to the spiritual, Madonna became a pop-cultural phenomenon in her own right—spawning legions of teenage "Madonna Wanna-bes" and scoring one pop hit after another throughout the eighties and nineties. Her most ambitious album, 1989's *Like a Prayer,* incorporated elements of pop, rock, and dance styles. The album hit number one and yielded the Top 10 singles "Like a Prayer," "Express Yourself," "Cherish," and "Keep It Together." With "Vogue" in 1990, Madonna continued to show her skill at imprinting appropriated musical styles with her own style. Scathing reviews for her 1992 steel-bound soft-core pornographic book *Sex,* featuring erotic photos of the singer and several models and celebrities, didn't prevent the accompanying album, *Erotica,* from selling more than two million copies.

Beginning with her Golden Globe–winning performance as Eva Peron in the 1995 film adaptation of Andrew Lloyd Webber's *Evita,* Madonna recast herself as a stylish sophisticate. The movie's soundtrack was a modest hit, with a dance remix of "Don't Cry for Me Argentina" and the newly written "You Must Love Me" becoming hit singles. Showing influences of styles like electronica, techno, trip-hop, and drum-and-bass, Madonna's critically acclaimed *Ray of Light* in 1998 updated her classic dance-pop sound for the late nineties and provided further proof that she was far and away the most popular dance-music artist of all time.

Madonna has been hugely successful with the kind of music that Julian Marsh, one of the best-known deejays in the U.S., likes to play. Marsh made his mark at gay clubs and circuit parties by playing what he calls "happy music." He explained, "Club music has gotten hard and not friendly. It's abusive music. Most deejays play bits and pieces of songs, they play dubbed versions of the songs—things that hint at the melody and hint at the words, but never get to it. I don't believe in that. I think people like words." Marsh's mixes tend to be a combination of European dance music he finds in his twice-weekly record hunts, remixes of songs like Erin Hamilton's "Dream Weaver," and often songs featuring Lonnie Gordon. This hasn't endeared him to the clubs where the hard-edged techno sound defines what they consider dance music. But the kind of music that Marsh plays is most welcome in the gay scene.

For decades, Provincetown, Massachusetts, the small town at the tip of Cape Cod, has been popular with gay vacationers, artists, and other free spirits. In P-town, the Boatslip has hosted a daily tea dance every summer for two decades, and the dance music played there gets wide exposure to a cross-section of gay people who then take the new sounds with them when they return home, literally across the country and around the world. Each day, from 3:30 to 6:30, the small dance floor and huge outdoor deck of the Boatslip become P-town's party central. Dancers thrust their arms exuberantly in the air to the strains of the newest and not-so-new divas as the beat drives them to a sweaty frenzy. On the sidelines, older men who survived the disco years stand in close quarters with the S & M ("stand and model") pretty boys who look out the corners of their eyes to see whether anyone has noticed them. The black JBL speakers suspended at each corner of the sunken dance floor pump out the sounds of summer madness. Above it all, the mirror ball turns.

For Labor Day 1999, the last big blowout of the summer

and the century, the Boatslip's dance mix included two of Whitney Houston's popular dance tracks, "It's Not Right" and "My Love Is Your Love"; Donna Summer's "I Will Go With You," off her just-released *Live and More: Encore;* Taylor Dayne's "Naked Without You"; Vicki Sue Robinson's "Move On"; Barbara Pennington's "24 Hours a Day"; the ABBA tribute group Abbacadabra's "SOS"; and, to close, Donna Summer's "Last Dance."

Diva-centrism for sure. But more than that are the words these divas sing—the simple fact of lyrics. Will Moppert, the former new-waver, runs the Boatslip's music shop. He notes that most people coming into the shop want dance music with a vocal track, and very few want techno. "I think it's a gay/straight thing," he said. "Gay men want happy music, fluffy music. Straight people only listen to club music when they go out dancing, whereas gay men have it in their cars, in their homes, it's part of their lifestyle."

But sexual orientation alone may not explain the reason these men enjoy dance music with words. "I think straight people like the vocals as much," says Maryalice Kalaghan, the Boatslip's deejay. "But the older anyone gets, the more they want the song." Maryalice, as she is known, notes that many clubs—and especially the rave dance parties that were popular among young people in the 1980s and 1990s—typically feature "deep house" without vocals and what she calls "hard, harsh" techno. This style of music appeals mainly to "club kids" barely old enough to drink legally. But, says Maryalice, "Thank God everyone gets older and they have to have the song!"

Whether it's because they grow to like the vocals, because they enjoy a more human touch, or simply because the gay clubs where they dance have always nurtured divas and their songs, many gay men have remained loyal to the disco divas and their brand of vocal dance music. Among gay dancers, "disco doesn't need to be resurrected," noted Barry Walters in a 1998 *Advocate* spread on the subject, "because to us it never died. It remains our soundtrack of life and liberation." He added, "You can bet you'll be hearing Sister Sledge's 'We Are Family' at every gay pride celebration this summer—and well into the twenty-first century."

Well before the beginning of the new century, however, we might have wondered what happened to the artists behind the disco music that once rocked the world. Some, the "one-hit wonders" of the disco years, are long since forgotten by all but true aficionados. Others continue to perform their disco hits in retro concerts for appreciative audiences, even attracting new fans among young people who were born around (or even after) the time that disco was in its prime. And those whose reputations were made in other musical formats before their forays into disco have simply moved on.

As the eighties got under way, disco artists were saying, like A Taste of Honey, "Rescue Me!" Many tried to adapt to the tastes of the new decade, but most of them simply faded into the magical mists from which they had emerged only a few years earlier. By 1986, most of the surviving disco groups had split, including in that year Boney M, Boystown Gang, and Kool and the Gang. Still other well-known disco artists became casualties of the AIDS epidemic, including Dan Hartman and Sylvester. Producer Jacques Morali, Paradise Garage deejay Larry Levan, and Academy Award–winning songwriter Paul Jabara were also among the many others known for making the music who perished in the AIDS epidemic along with tens of thousands of their fans.

Some of the artists whose music had become as much a

feature of nighttime as darkness itself simply moved on to the next phase of their own lives. Yvonne Elliman, whose number-one "If I Can't Have You" was featured in the *Saturday Night Fever* soundtrack, left her musical career to become a stay-at-home mom whose award-winning pies gave her the satisfaction that record making had once done. Sister Sledge continues to remake their hits in Europe, while sister Kathy Sledge occasionally records and performs live. Alicia "I Love the Nightlife" Bridges, the quintessential one-hit wonder of the disco era, now deejays occasionally at a club in Atlanta, where she and her female partner run a pet-grooming business.

In the summer of 1997, New York radio station WKTU sponsored an eight-hour, fifty-two-act show in Brooklyn. "Beatstock" featured dance music from 1975 to 1997, and some of the performers who originally recorded it. In that period WKTU itself had morphed from "mellow rock" to become the nation's number-one station when it adopted an all-disco format in 1978, and now it was offering a dance mix that the *New York Times*'s Jon Pareles described as featuring "pop melody, hip-hop swagger, a touch of funk, and, often, a dollop of Latin rhythm and percussion." Performers at the all-day dance fest included such disco names as Kathy Sledge, France Joli, Judy Tores, and Rochelle Fleming, representing the disbanded First Choice.

Other big-name artists of the disco years continue to perform, usually as retro acts. Two decades melted away in the fall of 1999, when Barry White and Earth, Wind & Fire performed at Washington, D.C.'s MCI Center. Although White sang his just-released "Staying Power," it was for "purring" his oldies—"Can't Get Enough of Your Love, Babe" and "You're the First, the Last, My Everything"—that the *Washington Post* praised him. Earth,

Wind & Fire's "solid rendition" of "Shining Star" was well received. "But," said the newspaper's reviewer, "such needless antics as the guitarist using his teeth to play his instrument were distracting." Clearly, the good humor with which the disco crowds of the seventies would have greeted "such needless antics" hadn't survived into the 1990s like the musicians themselves!

In the summer of 1999, disco queen Donna Summer released *Live and More: Encore!* (Sony/Columbia), another remake of some of her greatest hits. One cut off the album, a cover of "I Will Go with You" (originally recorded by Andrea Bocelli and Sarah Brightman) was extremely popular in the dance clubs that summer. Another of her new songs, "Ordinary Girl," was from an autobiographical musical, *Ordinary Girl,* co-written by and starring Summer herself. The show was to begin rehearsals after Summer's thirty-six-city 1999 tour from New York to California.

Today the woman marketed in the mid-seventies as "the First Lady of Lust" lives in Nashville, married for twenty years to Bruce Sudano, with whom she collaborated on the 1979 duet "Heaven Knows." Summer is the mother of three, and even has a granddaughter. Summer said little Vienna, at age two, was already a "diva in training." Summer has tried to make up to her many gay fans for the rumors of homophobia after a religious conversion by raising substantial amounts of money for AIDS organizations. And she is at peace with herself after reconciling herself to the status of "former" superstar. "My career is what I do for a living," she said. "My family and my friends and the people that I love—they are my life."

Twenty years after their own brief "moment," life is still busy for the still-popular, now-retro Village People. Felipe Rose, the group's Indian since its 1977 founding, says, "I can't complain. It's been very profitable for me. I've managed to make a career out of it. I've made a tremendous amount of money." Recalling his earlier career as a professional dancer—on everything from bars to the ballet stage—he said, "This is the longest job I've ever had, when you think about it."

Regularly touring in the U.S. and Europe, the costumed ones enjoyed a moment of sweet disco revenge in the summer of 1999. Almost twenty years to the day after the infamous "Disco Demolition" in Chicago's Comiskey Park, the Village People performed a twenty-minute set right on home base of the baseball stadium itself. "The irony of it all!" said Rose, noting that the fans now cheering them were perhaps descendants of the 1979 record-burners. "It was probably their parents or older brothers and sisters who said 'Disco sucks!' "

THE SECOND TIME AROUND

A revival of interest in disco music and styles was well under way in the U.S. at the end of the 1990s. "Disco is everywhere," said Gary A. Hemphill, who began *DiscoBeat* magazine in 1978 and is now a consultant to the beverage industry. "Even the grounds crew at the Yankee games dances to 'Y.M.C.A.' when they come out to rake the infield in the fifth inning. There's no escaping it." Jeff Olson, the Village People's cowboy since 1980, said the reason for the disco revival was simple. "The music is timeless," he said. "It's fun. So much of the music of the seventies dance era was based on fun."

As with the first disco explosion in 1978, though, the nation's second take on disco almost completely ignored the music's gay connections—even though the gay community had continued to support the music long after the public abandoned it. Barry Walters noted in *The Advocate,* "It's striking that as the once-dreaded disco resurfaces into mainstream consciousness via nostalgia, its ties to gay culture have been downplayed or denied altogether." Along with the Village People themselves, Walters said, "It's impossible not to contemplate what those millions of sports fans must be thinking as they do the 'Y.M.C.A.' dance every time the Village People's infamous ode to gay promiscuity is played during halftime."

On the other hand, and in the generous spirit of disco, we might allow that perhaps in dancing the Y.M.C.A., those fans were simply letting themselves forget for a moment that the Village People were gay icons and that so many expect everyone to label themselves one way or the other and stick to "their own." Very likely the increased openness of gay people in the cultural mainstream helped. But straight fans in the late seventies were certainly willing to accept the Village People as ambassadors of fun when the band was on the radio and selling tens of millions of records. Perhaps they were simply doing so again.

In the neo-disco revival of the 1990s, there were a host of places to hear classic disco music, as large and small nightspots throughout the country once again programmed it, at least occasionally. Disco didn't become an all-day, every-day fad as it was in the seventies, but it could be found with little effort. At Miami's Bermuda Bar, "Funk Dat Disco!" Sunday nights included staff dressed in disco fashions—platform shoes, afros, bell-bottoms—and even sometimes reenacting scenes from *Saturday Night Fever.* In Tempe, Arizona, there was live disco every Sunday night at Gibson's and Monday nights at The Rock. In San Jose, California, "The Groove" happened every Wednesday at The Usual. In Boca Raton, Florida, Polly Esther's featured a "disco inferno" on Fridays and Saturdays, and the unlikely combination of 1970s rock and disco on Sundays. Near the University of Iowa campus in Iowa City, there was a weekly disco night at the Union Bar & Grill. And in Ann Arbor, Michigan, on Wednesday nights you could get in free if you wore disco gear to The Nectarine.

For baby boomers seeking to meet others like themselves in Manhattan, there was Decade, a nightclub for the middle-aged featuring an elegant menu, a four-thousand bottle wine cellar, and late-seventies music like Evelyn "Champagne" King's "Shame" and Gloria Gaynor's "I Will Survive." Fifty-one-year-old Bobby Zarin, a real estate investor and owner of Zarin Fabrics in downtown Manhattan, on the dating circuit during a separation, said Decade was ideal for people of a certain age and income level. "At Decade," he explained, "you have food, plenty of people in my age bracket that now have money to spend. This club is not dealing with kids who have no money." Underscoring the nostalgia behind Decade's concept, he added, "You have the music of my generation in a nice atmosphere."

For members of that generation (and others) who preferred a real seventies-style experience of the decade's music, there were still roller rinks like the Skate Palace in Temple Hills, Maryland, offering 1970s music nights. Every Thursday night, hundreds of mostly black adults paid an eight-dollar admission to zip around the rink to the music of their youth. The Skate Palace is one rink in a circuit of skating parties for Washington, D.C.–Baltimore-area people in their thirties and forties. The parties draw skating enthusiasts from the entire mid-Atlantic region.

Rande Hoggard, director of marketing for the Roller Skating Association International, said the "retro craze" had led to a resurgence of interest in roller-skating. "Bell-bottoms are back," said Hoggard, "and roller-skating on quad skates is back." Noting that the skating parties appealed mainly to African-Americans, management consultant and skating enthusiast Greg "Mac" McPhail, forty-one, said, "Most of the people who do this are from the inner city." They loved the music and they liked to move to it. Said McPhail, "I've been to skating parties that are majority white, and people just roll around the rink. They could care less about the music."

Disco music remained popular throughout the world, despite the greater preference for techno styles of dance music in clubs that considered themselves the hippest. The latest electronic fad in Japan in 1999 found schoolchildren and dark-suited "salarymen" lined up outside video arcades to pay three hundred yen (about $2.60) for the pleasure of disco dancing with a video game called Dance Dance Revolution. To the tunes of disco classics like K.C. and the Sunshine Band's "That's the Way (I Like It)," dancers moved on a raised platform covered with colorful flashing light panels, like an electronic Twister. The point was to follow the beat and match your steps to the time of the flashing squares. Dancers struck John Travolta poses and provided free entertainment for the amused crowds that gathered to watch them. One adventurous dancer said, "I've never been to a nightclub, but I've been here one hundred times." He had recently spent more than $260 on Dance Dance Revolution. "Now I've gotten used to people watching me," he said, "so maybe now I'll give nightclubs a try."

For those whose biggest regret in life was that they never got to dance in—or were turned away from—the original Studio 54, the Las Vegas MGM Grand in winter 1998 opened a three-story nightclub called—what else?—Studio 54. It featured a massive twenty-two thousand square feet of space, four separate dance floors and bars, an exclusive VIP guest area, semi-private lounges that could hold four hundred, artwork, and even paparazzi photographs from the original Studio 54.

Despite this kind of excess in the name of nostalgia, the excesses of the 1970s were disparaged regularly in the 1990s in almost any discussion of the earlier decade, whether in reference to its sex, drugs, or music. Looking back across the bleakness of AIDS and the button-down sensibility of the 1980s, many see the seventies as an idealized, innocent time when everything seemed possible and nothing was off limits. This selective memory played out in the latest disco fad, however scaled back the fad was by seventies standards. "Disco," said Peter Braunstein in a *Village Voice* article on the fad's origins, "can only be processed through the filter of nostalgia so that it comes out as a kitschy aesthetic with accompanying soundtrack." Braunstein noted that an important ingredient of what made disco "disco" is missing. "What's lost," he wrote, "is what made disco so alluring and threatening at the time: its heedless, unrepentant approach to pleasure."

What passes for disco in the mainstream nowadays is little more than the same handful of hits played repeatedly, and the fashions of the 1970s. Bernie Lopez of discomusic.com says he has been upset by these "really bad stereotypes of disco." He explained, "It seems as if, especially among the younger kids, their impression of disco is platform shoes and the same ten songs over and over again." This picking and choosing of what is to be remembered about a decade may be natural, but it doesn't give an accurate picture of the decade and the popular culture of the time. It celebrates the trappings of disco while ignoring the hard times of the 1970s that made the good times disco promised so very good. "Especially the younger generation," said Lopez, "who weren't there tend to glamorize it. People have these little icons and then they blow them way out of proportion. I think that's what happened with bell-bottoms and platform shoes."

For many, noted Amy M. Spindler in a *New York Times* article entitled "The Decade That Won't Go Away," the 1970s "epitomize bad taste, evoking a wasteland of synthetic disco clothing and avocado-and-gold kitchens." But, she reported, "For today's elite style-setters, the era continues to exert an almost magnetic appeal." Gucci designer Tom Ford, who began reviving 1970s styles as early as 1992, said, "Everything new happening in music, art, furniture design, and fashion design has these references." Ford attributed the borrowing from disco culture to an essentially unexciting historic period. The disco revival, he said, happened "because this generation hasn't had a dramatic life change. Going to the moon was a breakthrough. Ending the war was a breakthrough." Ford concluded on an unsettling note, observing that "Maybe we've hit a period like the Egyptians did where style stays the same for the next two thousand years."

If looking ahead two millennia is more than most of us are interested in doing, looking back two decades has become the obsession of more than a few of those driving today's popular culture via advertising, television, radio, the Internet, movies, and theater. Nostalgia is rife in an era less known for originality than for sampling and deriving its culture from earlier times. Even usually innovative Madonna remade Don McLean's early 1970s ode to rock and roll, "American Pie," in 2000. While the media had once promoted the disco trend, they now traffick in memories. Even if not a cultural temblor of the same magnitude as 1978's, disco is woven into today's popular culture in ways that are more subtle—no longer is it all day, every day—and play into America's national penchant for wanting to reclaim its lost innocence.

Of course, the "innocence" the 1990s longed for in recalling the 1970s was considerably different than the earlier decade's own nostalgic revival of the 1950s. The seventies longed for the comforts of homemaker moms, families that stayed together, a booming post-war economy, and a war-hero president who didn't feel obliged to point out that he was not a crook. In contrast, the 1990s revival of disco and the seventies represented a longing for the "innocence" of sex without the risk of death, drug use without the White House inveighing against it, and dance music that was only about good times. Compared to the devastation of AIDS alone, the belief that the seventies represented a kind of pre-lapsarian "innocence" was certainly an appealing, if naive, way to remember the decade.

So we were fed the sugar-coated stereotypes of a decade that puzzles so many with its seeming contradictions. Advertising sampled the fashions and the music, stripping them of their cultural and historic contexts and shamelessly playing the nostalgia card. There was the skinny young man in unisex-looking seventies-style nylon bikini underwear peering out of a group of models mostly dressed in black in a year 2000 Gucci magazine ad. Isaac Hayes's "Theme from *Shaft*" was being used to sell the Mitsubishi Spyder—whitewashed of the song's role in the blaxploitation film of the early seventies and its ground-breaking description of ghetto experience and assertion of black pride in popular music. The movie *Shaft* itself was remade in 2000, starring Samuel L. Jackson as the ultracool detective. Donna Summer's "Hot Stuff" was used to sell Whoppers, decidedly not the kind of beef the chanteuse had in mind in 1979, when the song was a number-one hit.

On television, Fox's *That Seventies Show* was renewed for two more seasons in 2000 after becoming the network's most-watched Tuesday night show. *That Seventies Show* portrayed high-school life in Wisconsin between 1976 and 1980, the actual high-school years of producer Mark Brazill, whose alter ego in the show was Eric Forman. Although the show was called "irresponsible" for depicting the gang of teenage pals smoking pot in the Forman basement, it also tackled the social shifts of the time in such heavier subjects as feminism, unemployment, and birth control. The show's costumes and wardrobe won an Emmy in 2000, the reward for its accurate portrayal of the styles of the time. Said Brazill, "It's harder than your average sitcom. You've got to go to thrift shops and go to Ebay, and you have to search and really commit to the period."

Disco music was widely available on radio stations as increasing numbers of radio stations beginning in the late 1990s programmed disco music from the seventies. By the end of 1999, radio stations featuring songs by black artists—R & B, hip-hop, and oldies (especially from the 1970s)—were the most popular music stations in the nation's largest cities. These stations were all classified as "R & B/Urban," the new shorthand for black music styles. What was called the "Jammin' Oldies" format featured upbeat funk and disco music by black artists of the seventies such as Earth, Wind & Fire, Barry White, and Kool and the Gang. Unlike black oldies stations, which tended toward Motown tunes and sought a mostly black audience, Jammin' Oldies stations targeted white and Spanish-speaking, as well as black, listeners. "The biggest hits on radio now are from artists that both young African-American kids and suburban kids enjoy," said Steve Hegwood, vice president of programming for the Lanham, Maryland–based Radio One chain of stations. What's more, recordings by black artists were now the nation's top sellers, having surpassed country artists in 1998.

For millions throughout the world, disco music retains its power, the compelling beat for the feet. The Internet provides an international web of listeners, dancers, and fans with dozens of Web sites devoted to every aspect of the disco era, from individual artists to disco fashions to downloadable disco hits. The Web site discomusic.com itself reflects the rise of disco nostalgia. What had started as Bernie Lopez's hobby, Bernie's Disco Music Page, suddenly attracted underwriting from record and book companies that realized the potential market he was tapping into and helped transform his homemade site into a full-service e-business.

If there is money to be made on nostalgia, Hollywood heads the line of those wanting to make it. So it was no surprise to see several disco movies appear in the late nineties. Attempting to re-create in authentic detail the mood and madness of the time, the movies used the disco club scene and music as a shorthand way to evoke the period. Unfortunately, they mostly chose to look back at the times through the rosy-eyed nostalgia of the nineties.

The first out was *Boogie Nights* in 1997, a chronicle of the Los Angeles porn industry from 1977 to 1984. Hip-huggers, shag haircuts, and a disco soundtrack faithfully re-created the era. We follow the rise and fall of busboy Eddie Adams, played by Mark Wahlberg (formerly known as Marky Mark), whose larger-than-life talent transforms him into Dirk Diggler, a hot property in the "adult entertainment" world. Casual sex and even more casual violence are everywhere in this well-made exploration of the sexual revolution's seamier sides. Like the best 1970s disco movies, the disco scene and music are backdrops for the characters' lives. But the music is forced to help symbolize the presumed moral vacuity of the era—rather than to be "about" the fun and liberation that it actually represented to those who enjoyed it in the seventies.

Just as the quality and plausibility of 1970s-era disco movies unraveled as the movies focused more and more on the disco world itself, it happened again with two 1998 movies that tried, each in its way, to re-create the aura of Studio 54. Whit Stillman's *Last Days of Disco* featured another soundtrack of disco's greatest hits, a Studio 54–like club in Manhattan, and a group of pretentious, heterosexual up-and-comers who somehow manage to get into the club. That alone was odd, as the actual Studio 54 would likely have turned them away, as it did with other straight, young singles—the "scurve," as they were known in club parlance. Over the din of the music, they discuss such profundities as whether their generation's interest in environmental causes stemmed from the revival of *Bambi* during their formative years.

The best part of the movie was the disco setting itself and of course the music—including such chestnuts as Carol Douglas's "Doctor's Orders," the Andrea True Connection's "More, More, More," Amii Stewart's "Knock on Wood," and the Michael Zager Band's "Let's All Chant." The movie ends on a surreal note with everyone in the New York subway system breaking into a choreographed riff on the O'Jays' "Love Train," and an even more surreal expostulation on the meaning of disco.

Also in 1998, writer and director Mark Christopher gave the world *54*. The "timid, meandering film," as the *New York Times* put it, featured comedian Mike Myers portraying Studio 54 co-owner Steve Rubell as a coked-out buffoon. Ryan Phillippe played a nineteen-year-old nobody from New Jersey who finds his destiny as a bartender at Studio 54, where he provides drugs to celebrities and keeps the boss's secrets. The movie featured another greatest-hits-of-disco soundtrack, and even Thelma Houston as herself singing a Christmas song. Speaking of *54* and *The Last Days of Disco*, Stephen Holden, the *Times* reviewer, said, "Sex, drugs, and disco: you couldn't ask for a juicier mix. But when it comes to squeezing juice, both movies come out dry."

The most anticipated arrival on the retro cultural scene was another multimillion-dollar production: the adaptation of *Saturday Night Fever* to the musical stage. Given the movie's tremendous success and the hundreds of millions it earned for the Robert Stigwood Organization, it wasn't surprising the show's producer would try to cash in on the disco-nostalgia craze with a remake of the most financially successful and famous disco property ever created. The four-million-pound show opened in London on May 5, 1998, and was not well received by the critics—though, as with critically savaged disco movies from the seventies, it proved quite popular.

The show was even less welcome to the critics in New York when it opened there on October 21, 1999. Despite the fourteen million dollars in advance ticket sales, said *New York Times* theater critic Ben Brantley, "It's hard to imagine any theatergoer finding much enjoyment in this hapless, robotic show." He elaborated, "The evening passes by as a joyless succession of flat words, sounds, and images that at best trigger memories of the vitality of the film that inspired it." In the *Daily News,* Fintan O'Toole concluded, "*Saturday Night Fever* feels more like a slight chill on a wet Tuesday evening."

James Carpinello, as Tony Manero, was as sexy an Italian-American and nimble a dancer as could be hoped for. The entire cast was made up of amazing dancers, their energy and precision to be marveled at. The packed Minskoff Theatre erupted regularly with appreciative applause. If the classic American story behind *Saturday Night Fever* got lost in the razzle-dazzle of the stage show, no one seemed to mind. Broadway in the age of Disney prefers its shows to be candy-coated musical spectacles. So the show tried to compensate for its soft center by jacking up the volume and wowing audiences with discofied production numbers to rival the show-stopping dance scenes of old Hollywood movies.

Lending further proof of the Disneyfication of Broadway, the Web site promoting *Saturday Night Fever* included this caveat: "The stage musical has been adapted and is suitable for all the family, there will be no foul language, drug usage, or violence against women." The culture-changing power of the movie soundtrack was diluted by putting the songs in the mouths of the actors themselves. The Bee Gees' falsettos and Tony Manero's hunger for escape were replaced by perfect diction and a kind of karaoke parody. Which isn't to say the show didn't have its catchy tunes, though they were mainly the new ones composed specially for the musical, such as the ballad "Immortality" and the rock-and-rolling "It's My Neighborhood."

The hits from the original movie by the original artists were like sticks of cultural dynamite in 1977 and 1978 that exploded onto the airwaves and into the nation's awareness. The music was natural to the 1977 movie because it simply was the music of that particular era. But the characters singing "their" songs reduced their individual stories to the song lyrics. In the show, for example, Tony Manero's spurned suitor Annette sings "If I Can't Have You." The song becomes her personal theme, rather than one of the themes of the story itself, as it was when Yvonne Elliman's version of the song recurred like a leitmotif throughout the movie, reinforcing the point that even the fondest dreams can remain elusive. As happened with the disco movies made after the original *Saturday Night Fever,* the musical wanted us to look at disco as a spectacle, rather than see the music and culture as part of the backdrop of an interesting, realistic story.

It was inevitable that the opening of *Saturday Night Fever* would spawn even more nostalgia for all things disco. In New York, Bloomingdale's opened a new *Saturday Night Fever* boutique to cater to everyone willing to spend $815 for a reproduction of John Travolta's famous white three-piece suit, or who felt the need for the assorted other kitschy retro fashions for sale. Among the items being offered—and seeming to appeal mainly to teens—was a sixty-eight-dollar asymmetrical skirt, a forty-two-dollar gunmetal sequined stretch tube top, and a dark denim jacket—eighty-eight dollars for women, ninety-eight dollars for men—created by Tommy Hilfiger that said NIGHT FEVER on the back.

Kal Ruttenstein, the store's fashion director, expected the boutique to attract "twentysomethings, thirtysomethings, and even fortysomethings who were there to experience the Studio 54 days firsthand." To anyone who might balk at the very notion, Ruttenstein said the new disco duds weren't really "retro" because "they're sleeker and more modern." He explained, "They're made with newer stretch fabrics, so they move when you dance. It's a dance collection for the millennium." Strangely, firsthand examination of the Bloomie's *Saturday Night Fever* men's collection turned up nothing more than a rack of overpriced cheap-feeling polyester suits stuck in a corner of the men's department. Far from being clothing for the millennium, they looked suspiciously like a rack of prom suits in a budget tux shop circa 1977.

Whether it was at the doors of Studio 54 in 1977, its first year, or at a new club starting up in Manhattan twenty-two years later, one thing was as constant as human nature itself: the craving for a sense of exclusivity, the need to feel that one "belongs" while other, lesser mortals do not. "For the first time in recent memory," reported *The New Yorker* in November 1999, a new club was opening in New York "without the benefit of a velvet rope." At least not an actual velvet rope. Rockstar Loft wasn't to be a regular nightclub with a front door and a cover charge. The monthly party, to be held somewhere on the West Side of Manhattan, would have a secret address and no admission cost.

The brainchild of three expatriate Englishmen, the club was promoted in downtown Manhattan in flyers and on a Web site listing a phone number of a voice mailbox. Three full-time staff members returned all the calls, asking each applicant to answer seven questions: (1) How did you hear about Rockstar Loft? (2) Why do you want to go? (3) If you could take someone, who would it be? (4) What is it you don't enjoy about current nightlife in New York? (5) What's the best movie you've seen in the last two years? (6) Who is your favorite deejay? (7) What has been the best moment in your life so far?

The answers were fed into a computer, then reviewed by

the proprietors. Naturally they had their own ideas about right and wrong answers based on their particular tastes. Appealing to the traditional biases that gain quick admission to a club— being a celebrity or knowing someone who knows someone— didn't work. "The worst thing people can say is 'I'm so-and-so, and I own this company, or run this record label, so I deserve to be invited,' " said co-proprietor Sam Houser. "We've made a lot of those people very angry." By the time the club opened, several thousand people had been winnowed to five hundred invites. The process would be repeated each month. Said another of the proprietors, Terry Donovan, "It really is a fascinating experiment in social engineering."

In reality, it was simply another example of the desire of those with a concept for a club to control the terms and conditions of their own nighttime fantasy. Steve Rubell used the terms "tossing a salad" and "painting a picture" for the way he handpicked the night's crowd at Studio 54. The young men controlling admission to Rockstar Loft called their own version of exclusivity "populist elitism." Many could apply, but few would be chosen.

In Berlin, reborn again as the German national capital and long a breeding ground of the underground music scene, Ed Ward reported in early 1999 that "the once-monolithic techno" scene had long since shattered, record sales were flat, and there was no longer any "underground" center to the scene. E-Werk, an old power plant in what used to be East Berlin that became an important techno club, had already been closed for two years. Love Parade, a formerly underground music festival, had now become a major annual pop event attracting two million people from everywhere in Europe. "It's the nature of undergrounds," Ward noted in the *New York Times,* "especially those that flourish, to become mainstream."

Of course disco music started as an underground taste in the early 1970s. Black people, gay men, and working-class folk who each had their own reasons for wanting to escape the mainstream whenever possible found their freedom in the discos. But then the Bee Gees, *Saturday Night Fever,* and Studio 54 showed the general public what fun and pleasure the music and the scene offered. What began as an underground movement became a commercial fad in the mainstream of popular culture. It was a cycle as old as humanity itself, and unlikely to change anytime soon.

After disco music had fulfilled so many needs, it was equally unlikely the basic dance-music formula—especially that four-on-the-floor beat—would soon be replaced. Nevertheless, it was impressive at the turn of the millennium to behold the way the best of the dance-club divas were still improving on and even innovating within the framework of disco-style music—and scoring major hits in the mainstream. In February 1999, Madonna's *Ray of Light* won Grammy Awards for both dance recording and pop album, a feat that would have done Donna Summer proud during her own peak twenty years earlier. The video for the album's title cut featured speeding images of a retro-looking forty-year-old Madonna punctuating an urban landscape and a discotheque that even had a 1970s-style lighted disco dance floor.

In the last year of the millennium, Cher was back with the megaselling album *Believe.* With a career of thirty-five years behind her, Cher's music was still burning up the airwaves and tearing up dance floors worldwide. Although she was reportedly opposed to making a disco album—even "neo-disco," as *Believe* was described—Cher doubtlessly thanked her producers (and her lucky stars) for mixing it up in the studio and giving her a huge hit—and a whole new generation of fans to boot. After making the usual snide jokes about Cher's durability, *Washington Post* reviewer Mike Joyce conceded, "It's hard to knock the way the album's producers [Mark Taylor, Brian Rawling, and Twilo deejay Junior Vasquez] have groomed her as a high-tech, electronica-age cousin of Gloria Gaynor and Donna Summer."

Perhaps there was no one better than Cher to epitomize the reasons why classic disco music was enjoying another upswing, even if the latest epidemic of disco fever was more a series of hot flashes than an inferno. Will Moppert, a "big Cher fan" since he was a boy, said, "What other artist has stayed in the mainstream since 1965 with 'I Got You, Babe' and has a number-one hit right now in 1999—and has made five major motion pictures in between, wrote exercise books, had a perfume, did infomercials, had a mail-order catalog of Gothic and medieval furniture? She's done everything known to man! And she's still here and she's still in the spotlight now more than ever before."

Already triple platinum within months of its release, *Believe* struck the right chord at the right time. Once again the singer had reinvented herself perfectly for the precise moment. With *Saturday Night Fever* on Broadway, Bloomingdale's once again running a disco boutique, and the Village People performing on the very spot where disco records were torched twenty years earlier, the timing was brilliant.

Cher's career spanned far more years than most of her newest fans had actually lived. Yet there they were, thousands of young and not-so-young Cher fans shrieking and dancing to the legendary singer's "new" disco music in a live concert broadcast on HBO from the MGM Grand in Las Vegas on August 29, 1999. When the fifty-three-year-old diva strutted onto the stage in an asymetrically cut red wig and black bell-bottoms—mirror balls suspended around the stage, backup dancers in multihued "disco wigs"—and sang "I'm Strong Enough," she erased every generation gap and brought everyone to their feet. Fans who grew up on Cher danced alongside more recent converts who may not have even heard of Cher before *Believe.* The show was an entertainment extravaganza, exciting to all the senses.

That is what disco was all about. It united everyone, young and old, straight and gay, black and white, male and female—whatever our label or subcategory of humanity—in the democracy of pleasure. As deejay Tony Moran, who produced seven tracks on Gloria Estefan's own 1998 disco-inspired album *Gloria!,* put it, "I just think that disco is sort of syncing up with the energy of the world. The most wonderful thing about dance music is what it inspires. It inspires us to smile and dance."

Today we have the great classic disco of the 1970s, rap and hip-hop, electronic dance music in its many forms, and four-on-the-floor dance-pop music that is really disco but wants to be called dance music. We've got the fashions, for better or worse. We even have movies and stage shows about disco's golden years.

But we can never really have "disco" again.

Disco was a moment in time. The stars were aligned just so. Politics and economics were grimmer businesses than usual. Sexual mores were in a state of flux. America was searching for its proper role as a superpower in a nuclear-armed world. In response to all of it, R & B singers from the New World got together with cutting-edge electronic soundmakers from the Old World to make dance music like no one had ever heard before.

And the people danced like there was no tomorrow. At the time, many didn't care to think about tomorrow. They wanted good times, and they found them in the fun and sexiness and silliness of disco.

All these years later, disco music—whether "retro" or "neo"—still moves us and we still listen to it because it speaks to two of our deepest, most primal needs: the need to play and the need to dance. Disco taught us to take those needs seriously.

TOP DISCO ARTISTS AND
THEIR HITS

Slide drums sliding, horns honking, definitely in a groove, Stevie Wonder sings out about just what it is that makes a hot song hot. In his own disco hit he sang, "Just because a record's got a groove don't make it in the groove. But you can tell right away it's got an 'A' if the people start to move!" How do you know a hot dance song? "You can feel it all over!" says Wonder. It moves you. It shakes you up. The song's lyrics might touch you or titillate you. One way or another, they get you all stirred up inside. And with a beat like a racing heart—your own heart racing from the adrenaline rush—your body is going to shout "Dance!"

Shaking things up and helping folks to get down—that's what disco music was all about. Here are brief biographies and discographies of the leading artists who made the music that made the people dance. Some of them made it big, others made a brief splash but gave disco a lasting legacy in their one hit. All of them contributed their creative talent and energy to the music behind the disco craze of the seventies. Many of them are still entertaining appreciative fans today in disco-music collections and "retro" performances.

A

ABBA

Considered the rock megagroup's only true disco song, as well as being the first twelve-inch ABBA single issued in the U.S., "Dancing Queen" (*Arrival*, Atlantic, 1977) was also the group's only song to hit number one in the U.S. Two other big dance favorites were "Lay All Your Love on Me" and "On and On and On," both off their 1980 album *Super Trouper* (Atlantic).

AMANT

Discomusic.com creator Bernie Lopez says of this Euro-disco style group's one major hit, "If There's Love" (*Amant*, Marlin, 1978), "What an awesome song even after all these years."

ANDREA TRUE CONNECTION

The adult-movie actress turned disco singer's "More, More, More" (*More, More, More*, Buddah, 1976) peaked at number four, while the very danceable "Party Line" from the same album didn't rise above number eighty.

AVERAGE WHITE BAND

The Scottish band was more funk than disco, but produced two "discoesque" hit singles in the mid-1970s, "Pick Up the Pieces" (*AWB* Atlantic, 1974) and "Cut the Cake" (*Cut the Cake*, Atlantic, 1975).

B

CLAUDJA BARRY

"Dancin' Fever" (*Claudja,* Salsoul, 1978) and "Boogie Woogie Dancin' Shoes" (*Boogie Woogie Dancin' Shoes,* Chrysalis, 1979) were her fun but only modestly successful disco songs, peaking respectively at numbers seventy-two and fifty-six.

THE BEE GEES

The rock group that became synonymous with disco music had an amazing streak of success in the late seventies. Putting their falsetto vocals to new use, the Gibb brothers were put on the disco map with their number-one singles "Jive Talkin' " (*Main Course,* RSO, 1975) and "You Should Be Dancing" (*Children of the World,* RSO, 1976). Then came the extraordinary success of the *Saturday Night Fever* soundtrack, with the group performing five of their original songs—"Stayin' Alive," "How Deep Is Your Love," "Night Fever," "More Than a Woman," and "You Should Be Dancing." Three of the songs ("How Deep Is Your Love," "Stayin' Alive," and "Night Fever") reached number one. A fourth, "If I Can't Have You," performed by Yvonne Elliman, also hit the top slot. In 1979, the group hit the top for the last time in the disco years with "Tragedy" and "Love You Inside Out" (*Spirits Having Flown,* RSO, 1979.).

BELL & JAMES

Leroy Bell, nephew of famed producer Thom Bell, and Casey James had one gold single in "Livin' It Up (Friday Night)" (*Bell & James,* A&M, 1979), which peaked at number fifteen, and did little to follow up their initial success.

BLONDIE

The New York–based new wave/pop/rock band, formed in 1975, had limited success in the U.S. until their disco song "Heart of Glass" (*Parallel Lines,* Chrysalis, 1978) hit number one. Blondie reached number one two more times with "Rapture" (*Autoamerican,* Chrysalis, 1980) and "Call Me" (*The Best of Blondie,* Chrysalis, 1981) before the group broke up and the disco era ended.

BOYSTOWN GANG

Hailing and drawing their gay sensibility from San Francisco, this latter-day disco group emulated the Village People in more ways than one. Like the costumed ones, the gang successfully crossed into the mainstream. Also like them, Boystown Gang started as a studio band put together by producer Bill Motley to record "Remember Me/Ain't No Mountain High Enough" as a tribute to Diana Ross and Motown. While the single was a club and chart hit, it was the B side that got attention. The thirteen-minute "Cruisin' the Street" was a gay porno fantasy with far racier language than virtually anything else commercially available at the time. Remaking 1960s pop love ballads into disco remixes, the gang was known for its Hi-NRG West Coast disco takes on Stevie Wonder's "Signed, Sealed, Delivered (I'm Yours)" and the Four Seasons' "Can't Take My Eyes Off You" (*Can't Take My Eyes Off You,* ERC, 1982).

ALICIA BRIDGES

One of the best known of disco's "one-hit wonders," Bridges's hit "I Love the Nightlife" (*Alicia Bridges,* Polydor, 1978) went to number five on the *Billboard* charts in 1979. Bridges's craving for "ack-shun" in the song was quite different from her country-music origins, but she says she never regretted it. Her hit song had a new life when it was featured in the soundtrack of the 1996 Australian movie *Priscilla, Queen of the Desert*. Bridges says nothing makes her feel better than to see people dancing to the song she made more than twenty years ago. "It brings tears of joy to my eyes to this day," she said.

BROOKLYN DREAMS

This New York disco vocal group missed the Top 40 with their first single, "Music, Harmony, Rhythm" (Casablanca, 1977). But with "Heaven Knows," their duet with Donna Summer (*Sleepless Nights*, Casablanca, 1979), they made it to number one. In 1980, group member Bruce Sudano married Donna Summer.

PATTIE BROOKS

A former session singer turned disco singer, this Los Angeleno didn't chart a pop hit, but she did have a major disco hit in the single-sided "After Dark" (Casablanca, 1978). The song was featured in *Thank God It's Friday* and used as one of the movie's single-sided twelve-inch promotional records.

MIQUEL BROWN

Brown's only 1970s disco album, *Dancin' with the Lights Down Low*, included the title track as well as "The Day They Got Disco in Brazil." She was best known for her big dance single in disco's "last days," "So Many Men, So Little Time" (JSR, 1983).

PETER BROWN

His first major hit, "Do Ya Wanna Get Funky with Me" (*A Fantasy Love Affair*, Drive, 1977), was the first twelve-inch dance record to sell more than one million copies in the U.S. From the same album, "Dance with Me" peaked at number eight while "You Should Do It" peaked at number fifty-four.

(

IRENE CARA

Toward the end of the disco era, Irene Cara appeared in—and scored her first hit with the title track of—the 1980 movie *Fame*. She was back in 1983 with the hit "Flashdance (What a Feeling)" from the movie *Flashdance* (See *The Casablanca Records Story*, Casablanca, 1994). The following year, she starred in a comedy called *D.C. Cab*, then disappeared until releasing the 1997 single "All My Heart." She continues to record dance music in Europe.

CERRONE

The multitalented drummer, composer, producer, and vocalist was best known for one of the first full-side extended songs, "Love in C Minor" (*Love in C Minor*, Atlantic, 1976). His next album, *Cerrone's Paradise* (Atlantic, 1977), didn't sell as well but it does include a disco classic, "Take Me." Another Cerrone disco classic was "Supernature" off his third album, *Cerrone 3—Supernature* (Cotillion, 1978).

CHER

The fashion iconoclast, Oscar-winning actress, and musical chameleon had a brief disco stint with "Take Me Home" (*Take Me Home*, Casablanca, 1979). The song peaked at number eight. Twenty years later, Cher was hailed as a "disco queen for the 1990s" because of the extraordinary success of her "neo-disco" (as it was described) "Believe" (*Believe*, Warner Bros., 1998). *Believe* won Cher the Grammy for best dance recording at the Grammy Awards in February 2000.

CHIC

The stylish group could rightly be called one of disco's best "big bands" because of their smooth, classy sound. Chic reached number one twice, with one of the biggest disco hits ever (and Atlantic Records' top-selling single), "Le Freak" (*C'est Chic*, Atlantic, 1978), and another disco anthem, "Good Times" (*Risqué*, Atlantic, 1979). Written about Studio 54, "Le Freak" was a huge hit, selling six million copies in the U.S. alone, reigning in the number-one slot on the charts for six weeks. The group's other popular tunes include "Dance, Dance, Dance (Yowsah, Yowsah, Yowsah)" (from their debut album, *Chic*, Atlantic, 1977), the number-one "I Want Your Love" (also from *C'est Chic*), and "My Forbidden Lover" (from *Risqué*).

LINDA CLIFFORD

This Brooklyn-born former Miss New York State turned from jazz to disco, giving the genre (and the era) one of its defining tunes, "If My Friends Could See Me Now" (*If My Friends Could See Me Now*, Curtom, 1978). She also brought dancers on the floor with her "Runaway Love" (also on *If My Friends Could See Me Now*), a discofied remake of Simon and Garfunkel's "Bridge Over Troubled Water" (*Let Me Be Your Woman*, RSO, 1979), and "Red Light" (*I'm Yours*, RSO, 1980).

The Commodores

Led by the honeyed vocals of Lionel Richie, this Alabama-grown rhythm and blues group had many pop hits before making a transition to disco around 1977 with "Fancy Dancer" (*Hot on the Tracks*, Motown, 1976) and "Brick House" (*Commodores*, Motown, 1977). The group then moved toward a mellower, slower sound with songs like "Three Times a Lady" (*Natural High*, Motown, 1978) and "Still" (*Midnight Magic*, Motown, 1979), both of which reached number one.

Crown Heights Affair

A New York funk-disco band whose second album, *Dreaming a Dream* (De-Lite, 1975) yielded the disco classic "Dreaming a Dream (Goes Dancin')."

D

Rick Dees and His Cast of Idiots

Memphis deejay Rick Dees decided to parody disco music and wound up with a number-one hit and platinum seller. "Disco Duck (Part 1)" (*Disco Duck [Part 1]*, RSO, 1976) also had the distinction of being perhaps the most frequently burned disco record of the disco era. A follow-up, "Dis-Gorilla (Part 1)," (*Dis-Gorilla [Part 1]*, RSO, 1977) continued the mimicry but didn't go higher than number fifty-six on the charts.

The Destinations

This disco studio group recorded "I've Got to Dance" in 1976 on the Avi label. The B side of the single is an instrumental version of the song called "The Hustle and the Bus Stop." They had their biggest disco hit with their remake of Curtis Mayfield's "Move On Up" (Butterfly, 1979).

DR. BUZZARD'S ORIGINAL SAVANNAH BAND

Rolling Stone described the band's sound as "a remarkable fusion of disco, big-band jazz, and a gamut of Latin musical genres." Their first album, *Dr. Buzzard's Original Savannah Band* (RCA, 1976), is a classic of the disco era. It includes the group's best-known hits, "Cherchez la Femme" and "I'll Play the Fool."

CARL DOUGLAS

Jamaica native Douglas was reared in England and became the first British-based artist to top the American R & B charts when he reached number one with his 1975 hit "Kung Fu Fighting" (*Kung Fu Fighting and Other Great Love Songs*, 20th Century, 1974). Douglas explained how he came up with the song: "There was some record playing, I don't remember which, but there were quite a few young kids in there [a pinball alley in London's Soho] who were having a kind of mock fight in time to the music. I turned to the guy I was with and said, 'Damn, looks like everybody's kung fu fighting,' and at that moment, I heard it all in my head, melody line as well, so I had to rush home and write it down."

CAROL DOUGLAS

After leaving the Chantels in the early seventies, Douglas just missed the Top 10 (the song reached number eleven) with "Doctor's Orders" (*The Carol Douglas Album*, Midland International, 1975), one of the earliest and most durable of disco songs. Her follow-up album *Midnight Love Affair* (Midsong) did well in 1976. Her version of the Bee Gees' "Night Fever" reached the singles charts in the U.K. Douglas was last heard from in the early eighties with the single "You're Not So Hot."

EARTH, WIND & FIRE

The funky rhythm and blues–style band made it into the Top 40 sixteen times, beginning with the single "Love Is Life" off their debut album *Earth, Wind & Fire* (Warner Bros., 1971). In 1975, they hit number one with "Shining Star" (*That's the Way of the World,* Columbia). In 1978, the group won Grammys for best R & B group performance for "Shining Star" and "All 'n All," and for best R & B instrumental performance for "Runnin'." That year, *Rolling Stone* said the band put on "one of the most elaborate stage shows in rock and roll history." In 1979, the group teamed up with the Emotions to make the disco classic "Boogie Wonderland" (*I Am,* ARC/Columbia). Off the same album, "After the Love Has Gone" peaked at number two.

YVONNE ELLIMAN

After bursting onto the airwaves in 1970 with "I Don't Know How to Love Him," from *Jesus Christ Superstar,* Elliman released six albums between 1972 and 1979. She was best known for her *Saturday Night Fever* classic "If I Can't Have You" (*Night Flight,* RSO, 1978; also on the *Saturday Night Fever* soundtrack). Written by the Bee Gees and used throughout the movie, the song was one of the movie's multiple number-one hits. Another of

168 • TOP DISCO ARTISTS AND THEIR HITS

Elliman's popular club hits (though it only charted at number thirty-four) was "Love Pains" (*Yvonne*, RSO, 1979).

THE EMOTIONS

Jeanette, Sheila, and Wanda Hutchinson were known as the Heavenly Sunbeams when they started out as child gospel singers in the mid-1950s, later touring with the legendary Mahalia Jackson. In 1968, the sisters turned to rhythm and blues, and became the Emotions. The group scored their biggest hit—and a Grammy for best R & B performance—with 1977's "Best of My Love" (*Rejoice*, Columbia). *Billboard* called "Best of My Love" the most successful girl group song of the rock era. The Emotions also provided the backup vocals for "Boogie Wonderland," Earth, Wind & Fire's huge 1979 hit, and toured with the Commodores in the early 1980s.

F

FIRST CHOICE

Originally known as the Debronettes, this girl group was best known for their early disco hit "Armed and Extremely Dangerous" (*Armed and Extremely Dangerous,* Philly Groove, 1973). They had another popular club hit with "Doctor Love" (*Delusions,* Gold Mine/Salsoul, 1977).

THE FOUR SEASONS

After their huge success in the 1960s, the group reformed in 1975 to try their hand at disco. Again they succeeded with

"Who Loves You" (*Who Loves You,* Warner, 1975) and the number-one hit off the same album, "December 1963 (Oh What a Night)."

FOXY

The five-member Miami-based disco band had two albums and two hit singles, then pretty much disappeared. "Get Off (Your Ass and Dance)" (*Get Off,* Dash, 1978) charted at number nine and was one of the first songs to incorporate the "boop-boop" vocal sound characteristic of many 1970s disco records (the most famous being the Michael Zager Band's "Let's All Chant"). "Hot Number" (*Hot Numbers,* Dash, 1979) reached twenty-one on the U.S. charts.

G

GLORIA GAYNOR

Born in 1949 and raised in Newark, New Jersey, Gaynor was performing in jazz clubs and touring with a group called the Soul Satisfiers before she released her 1974 remake of the Jackson 5's "Never Can Say Goodbye" (*Never Can Say Goodbye,* MGM). New York club deejays in 1975 proclaimed Gaynor "Queen of the Discos." Yet she was nearly forgotten until re-emerging with the platinum 1978 hit "I Will Survive" (*Love Tracks,* Polydor). The single hit number one on March 3, 1979, and won a Grammy. That year Gaynor opened for the Village People on the first nationwide Disco Arena tour, playing at major stadiums.

Andy Gibb

The youngest brother—though never a member—of the Bee Gees, he became the first artist ever to reach number one with each of his first three singles, "I Just Want to Be Your Everything," "(Love Is) Thicker Than Water" (both from *Flowing Rivers*, RSO, 1977), and "Shadow Dancing" (*Shadow Dancing*, RSO, 1978). The songs were co-written with Gibb's older brothers. Gibb later hosted *Solid Gold* and starred in the Broadway production of *Joseph and the Amazing Technicolor Dreamcoat*. He died on March 10, 1988, at age thirty.

Gonzalez

This British disco band scored one hit, "Haven't Stopped Dancing Yet" (*Shipwrecked*, Capitol, 1979) before dropping out of the U.S. disco scene.

GQ

The Bronx-based group recorded earlier as the Rhythm Makers before their 1978 name change to GQ (for "Good Quality"). Their first album, *Disco Nights* (Arista, 1979), gave them their biggest hit, the classic of the same name.

H

Dan Hartman

After a stint as the bass player for rocker Edgar Winter, Hartman made the disco scene in 1978 with the now-classic "Instant Replay" (*Instant Replay*, Blue Sky, 1978). That year he also hit the charts with the rock song "Free Ride." Off the same album, "This Is It" didn't get any higher than number ninety-one. After this brief bit of success, Hartman produced other bands and bought a studio called the Schoolhouse. He also wrote for several other artists in the 1970s, including "Love Sensation" for Loleatta Holloway, on the Salsoul label. He was back on the charts in 1984 with "I Can Dream About You." His last album, *Keep the Fire Burning,* in 1994, included the radio hit "Relight My Fire" (Blue Sky), again featuring Loleatta Holloway. Hartman died from AIDS that same year.

ISAAC HAYES

The funk producer, songwriter, pianist, and vocalist had one of the earliest "disco" hits, the "Theme from *Shaft" (Shaft,* Enterprise, 1971). The song hit number one, and the soundtrack of the blaxploitation movie won the Academy Award. After forming his own Hot Buttered Soul record label in 1975, Hayes scored more hits in the late seventies. The single "Don't Let Go" (Polydor, 1979) peaked at number eighteen. Some disco aficionados feel that his best disco song of all, though it reached only number seventy-five, was "Zeke the Freak" (*For the Sake of Love,* Polydor, 1978).

HEATWAVE

Founded by Johnnie and Keith Wilder, two brothers from Dayton, Ohio, Heatwave started out in Europe in the mid-1970s with members hailing from much of the continent. One song on the group's 1976 debut album, *Too Hot to Handle* (Epic), got attention in the U.S., becoming an instant and enduring disco hit: "Boogie Nights." They made it into the Top 10 once more with "Groove Line" (*Central Heating,* Epic, 1978). During the group's 1978 U.S. tour, *Rolling Stone* critic Abe Peck said, "Athough Heatwave's music is far more imaginative than your typical foot-stomping disco drone, it's taken a tour of the U.S. for [Johnnie] Wilder and Heatwave to emerge from the Valley of the Disco Clones."

PATRICK HERNANDEZ

After "Born to Be Alive" (*Born to Be Alive,* Columbia) reached number sixteen in 1979, French-born Hernandez receded into memory, but his backup singer, Madonna, went on to become a phenomenon in her own right.

LOLEATTA HOLLOWAY

A soul singer in the early 1970s, Holloway was best known for her disco hits. After moving to Gold Mind Records (distributed by Salsoul) in 1977, she gave the world the disco classics "Hit and Run" (*Hit and Run,* Gold Mind, 1977) and, in 1980, "Love Sensation" (written by Dan Hartman). "Love Sensation" was covered in the 1980s by Black Box, whose version of the song was called "Ride on Time." In 1982, Holloway sang "Seconds" with the Salsoul Orchestra, produced by Patrick Adam (*Salsoul Orchestra Featuring Loleatta Holloway,* Salsoul, 1982).

THELMA HOUSTON

Soul singer Houston recorded seven albums (including six for Motown between 1972 and 1979), but it was "Don't Leave Me This Way" (*Don't Leave Me This Way,* Motown, 1976) that made it to number one—and defined her career. The song, a cover of the earlier version of the song by Harold Melvin and the Blue Notes, earned Houston a Grammy in 1977 for best female rhythm and blues vocal performance. *Billboard* nominated her for Top Disco Artist and Female Pop Artist of the Year. Her disco track "Love Masterpiece" (*Love Masterpiece*, Motown, 1978) was used in the film *Thank God It's Friday*. Said Houston, "I think disco is very underrated. Something very good is going on there. It gives good psychological lift to people."

HUES CORPORATION

Formed in 1969 and named for billionaire recluse Howard Hughes, this Los Angeles–based soul group didn't find their niche until the start of the disco era. They recorded the soundtrack for *Blacula* in 1972. Their debut album, *Freedom for the Stallion*, included the smash hit "Rock the Boat" (*Rock the Boat*, RCA, 1974), one of the first disco songs and widely credited with helping to usher in the disco era.

J

JACKSON 5

(Also see the Jacksons.) Hailing from Gary, Indiana, Jackie, Tito, Marlon, Jermaine, and Michael Jackson formed the Jackson 5 in 1966. The Jackson brothers first recorded for Motown in 1968. Their music was some of the liveliest in the years just before disco emerged, and in many ways they laid the groundwork for the genre. The group's funk-soul-rock style made them natural disco artists. "Dancing Machine" (*Dancing Machine*, Motown, 1974) is one of the great disco songs. In 1976 the group left Motown for Epic, and Jermaine Jackson—later, Michael Jackson, too—left for a solo career.

THE JACKSONS

(Also see Jackson 5.) When the Jackson 5 left Motown in 1976, they left their name with them. With Epic, they revived their careers with the platinum hit "Enjoy Yourself" (*Enjoy Yourself,* Epic, 1976). Two of their later disco tunes became classics, "Blame It On the Boogie" (*Blame It On the Boogie,* Epic, 1977) and "Shake Your Body (Down to the Ground)" (*Shake Your Body [Down to the Ground],* Epic, 1978).

MICHAEL JACKSON

From boy star of the Jackson 5, Michael shot to solo fame with his 1979 album *Off the Wall* (Epic), produced by the legendary Quincy Jones. The album reached number three and spawned four Top 10 hits. It yielded disco classics, including two number-one hits, "Don't Stop 'Til You Get Enough" and the title cut. Jackson followed up his success with the stunningly successful *Thriller* (Epic) in 1982, the best-selling album in history, with total sales of 46 million. The album includes the very danceable "Wanna Be Startin' Somethin'," "Thriller," and "Beat It."

RICK JAMES

Funk prodigy Rick James started his musical career in Toronto, where he played in the rock band Mynah Birds, which also featured Neil Young. James played bass with various groups before Motown signed him up in the late 1970s as a singer/songwriter/producer. His 1978 debut album, *Come and Get It!,* went gold thanks to the success of such singles as "You and I" and "Mary Jane." Frequently compared to Prince and George Clinton, James cranked out a string of hits including "Bustin' Out" (1979), "Give It to Me Baby" (1981), and the song for which he's best known, "Super Freak" (*Street Songs,* Gordy, 1981). He also produced albums by the Temptations, the Mary Jane Girls, and Teena Marie. By the end of the decade, James was struggling with personal issues, and his music was being upstaged by sampling rappers, including M. C. Hammer, whose "U Can't Touch This" in 1990 was a rap over a loop of "Super Freak."

FRANCE JOLI

This young Canadian singer is known for one disco track, "Come to Me" (*France Joli*, Prelude, 1978). The song peaked at number fifteen in the U.S. but was a huge hit in Europe.

GRACE JONES

Actress, model, reggae dance singer, and AIDS activist Grace Jones burst into the disco world in 1977 with her first album for Island Records, *Portfolio*. Her striking Afro-Caribbean looks and outrageous persona made Jones an adored figure in the night-club world. Her disco cover of Edith Piaf's classic "La Vie en Rose" (*Portfolio*) was an instant club hit and remains one of Jones's best-known tunes. Wildly popular among gay disco-goers, Jones played to her fans in songs like "I Need a Man" (also from *Portfolio*) and, later, "Pull Up to the Bumper" (*Nightclub-bing*, Island, 1981). She was more popular in the eighties than in the seventies, and her "Slave to the Rhythm" (*Island Life*, Island, 1985) pretty well summed up what disco was about. In 1992, she starred in Eddie Murphy's box-office success *Boomerang*. Her heyday, though, was the late seventies and early eighties, when, as *The Advocate* put it, "Grace was fabulousness itself."

PATRICK JUVET

Swiss-born Juvet was a big name of the so-called Euro-disco genre of electronic-laden disco music. Village People and Ritchie

Family producer Jacques Morali wrote many of Juvet's tunes. Although he never made it into the Top 100, his "I Love America" (*I Love America*, Casablanca, 1978) is a disco classic. Another of Juvet's disco favorites was "Got a Feeling" (*Got a Feeling*, Casablanca, 1979), which made the U.K. charts. Juvet's star set as the disco phenomenon was winding down, and his last album, sung in French, was *Sex et Drugs et Rock 'n Roll* (Virgin, 1979).

K

K.C. AND THE SUNSHINE BAND

Formed by Harry Wayne Casey and Richard Finch in 1973, K.C. and the Sunshine Band defined the Miami Sound of the 1970s. From their first hit, the debut single "Blow Your Whistle," the group was off and running on what would be a string of major hits. Casey and Finch helped spark the disco craze with the song they wrote for then-unknown George McCrae, the 1974 chart-topping "Rock Your Baby." A year later, the band itself was on top of the charts with their hits "Get Down Tonight" and "That's the Way (I Like It)" (both from *K.C. & the Sunshine Band*, TK, 1975). In the bicentennial year it was "(Shake, Shake, Shake) Shake Your Booty," and "I'm Your Boogie Man" (*K.C. & the Sunshine Band Part 3*, TK, 1976). The *Saturday Night Fever* soundtrack featured K.C.'s song "Boogie Shoes." By the time "Please Don't Go" was released in 1979, Casey and Finch already had more than five hundred published titles under their belt. But even with five number-one hits and four Grammy Awards to their credit, the group's only hit in the eighties was the dance classic "Give It Up" (*Give It Up*, Epic, 1983).

CHAKA KHAN

From 1973 to 1977, Chaka Khan sang with the funk group Rufus. The group won a Grammy in 1974 for best R & B performance by a group for their funk/disco hit "Tell Me Something Good." In 1978, Khan struck out on her own and scored with "I'm Every Woman" (*I'm Every Woman*, WEA, 1978; re-recorded by Whitney Houston for *The Bodyguard* soundtrack). She is probably best known for her 1984 hit "I Feel for You," written by the artist then known as Prince.

EVELYN "CHAMPAGNE" KING

Her big disco classic "Shame" reached number nine on the U.S. charts and went gold in the U.S. and double platinum worldwide. She also had a big dance hit in the U.K. with "Love Come Down" (*Love Come Down*, RCA, 1982), which appealed to a non-disco audience as the disco era was ending.

KOOL AND THE GANG

This R & B and soul group was put together in 1964 by Robert "Kool" Bell in Jersey City, New Jersey. Popular before and after the disco years, the group found a niche in disco. "Jungle Boogie" (*Wild and Peaceful*, De-Lite, 1973) was one of the group's first hits—and one of the earliest songs to cross from funk to disco. Their "Open Sesame" (*Open Sesame*, De-Lite, 1976) was featured in *Saturday Night Fever*. They were back in the Top 10 in 1979 with "Ladies' Night" and "Too Hot" (*Ladies Night*, De-Lite). They hit number one with their disco anthem "Celebration" (*Celebrate!*, De-Lite, 1980). Their last time in the Top 10 was with "Get Down on It" (*Something Special*, De-Lite, 1981), which squeaked in at number ten.

KRAFTWERK

Formed by two students from Düsseldorf, Germany, who met at a classical-music conservatory in 1968, Kraftwerk (German for "power plant") was a big name in Euro-disco. They had one significant U.S. hit with the 1976 song "Autobahn," twenty-two minutes of mechanical rhythms, monotone vocals, and electronic beeps.

L

LaBELLE

This girl group formed in Philadelphia in 1962 as the Blue Belles, with Patti LaBelle as the lead singer alongside Sarah Dash, Nona Hendryx, and Cindy Birdsong, who left to join the Supremes in 1967. Among their disco hits was the 1975 number one "Lady Marmalade" (*Nightbirds,* Epic, 1974), which brought the French expression "Voulez-vous coucher avec moi, ce soir?" into popular usage. Patti LaBelle left the group in 1976 to strike out on what became a highly successful solo career.

CHERYL LADD

The supermodel turned *Charlie's Angels* co-star recorded two disco albums. Only one song, "Think It Over" (*Cheryl Ladd,* Capitol, 1978), caught on. The other album was *Dance Forever* (Capitol, 1979).

LIPPS, INC.

This disco studio group, formed in Minneapolis in 1977, is remembered for its one major disco hit. Cynthia Johnson, who was crowned Miss Black Minnesota in 1976, sang the lead on

"Funkytown" (*Mouth to Mouth*, Casablanca, 1980). After that the group faded into obscurity.

LOVE AND KISSES

Brainchild of producer Alec Costandinos, the group's first LP, *Love and Kisses* (Barclay, 1977), actually contained only two songs, one of which was the notable "Accidental Lover," considered by connoisseurs to be a brilliant piece of Euro-disco. Their best-known hit was the title cut from the *Thank God It's Friday* soundtrack (Casablanca, 1978), which won the Academy Award for best movie soundtrack.

CHERYL LYNN

Los Angeles native Cheryl Lynn landed a recording contract with CBS Records after making it to the end of *The Gong Show* (performing "You Are So Beautiful") without being gonged off the stage. A Studio 54 favorite, her "Got to Be Real" (*Cheryl Lynn*, Columbia, 1978) was a huge disco smash. Off the same album, she also charted with "Star Love," then again two albums later with "Shake It Up Tonight" (*In the Night*, Columbia, 1981). She made a hit duet with Luther Vandross called "If This World Were Mine" and charted again in 1983 with "Encore."

M

KELLY MARIE

Her hopping dance tune "Feels Like I'm in Love" (*Feels Like I'm in Love*, Calibre, 1979) was the best-selling U.K. disco record of 1980, and a smash in gay clubs in the U.S. in 1981.

Van McCoy

Although the talented arranger and composer worked with such performers as the Shirelles, Aretha Franklin, Gladys Knight and the Pips, and the Stylistics, he is best known for his number-one gold single, the name of which became synonymous with disco. "The Hustle" (*The Hustle*, Avco, 1975) not only introduced synchronized ballroom-style dancing to disco music, but it won a Grammy in 1975 for best performance by an orchestra. It featured the Soul City Symphony, with vocals backed by brass, strings, a piccolo, and of course the beat that inspired the dance. The song was an instant international success, selling more than eight million copies worldwide. McCoy's subsequent disco songs didn't go far, though his last big hit in the U.K., "The Shuffle" (*The Shuffle*, H&L, 1977), was used as the theme for the BBC's Radio 4 sports report for nearly twenty years. McCoy died of a heart attack in 1979.

George McCrae

With background track and vocals by Harry Casey and Rick Finch of K.C. and the Sunshine Band, "Rock Your Baby" (*Rock Your Baby*, TK, 1974) was an international smash. Besides hitting number one, the song was one of the earliest commercially successful disco songs. Other than reaching number thirty-seven with "I Get Lifted" off the same album, McCrae's Top 40 hits in the U.S. were already over, though he went on to release a string of singles.

Gwen McCrae

Wife and singing partner of George McCrae, she reached number nine with "Rockin' Chair" (*Rockin' Chair*, Cat, 1975). Her only other chart hit was "Keep the Fire Burning" (Atlantic) in 1982.

McFadden & Whitehead

Among the duo's songwriting hits for Philadelphia International Records was the O'Jays' hit "Backstabbers," the first number-one hit for that group and for the record company. After finally persuading Philadelphia's Gamble and Huff to let them record a song of their own, Gene McFadden and John Whitehead thought to themselves (and told *Billboard*), "They're letting us go into the studio: ain't no stopping us now!" The album *McFadden & Whitehead* went gold in 1979, and the hit single "Ain't No Stoppin' Us Now" became a disco classic.

Harold Melvin and the Blue Notes

This Philadelphia International soul group had been around, in one form or another, since the late 1950s. But they had their biggest success with the number-one hit "If You Don't Know Me by Now" (*If You Don't Know Me by Now*, CBS, 1973). Their follow-up song, "The Love I Lost" (*The Love I Lost*, Philadelphia International, 1974), was one of the transitional songs marking the emergence of disco from traditional rhythm and blues as a distinctive style of music. The group recorded "Don't Leave Me This Way" (*Don't Leave Me This Way*, Philadelphia International, 1977) before Thelma Houston reached number one with her remake of it.

M.F.S.B.

Mother, Father, Sister, Brother, M.F.S.B. for short, was the house band for Philadelphia International Records. They performed a number of hits by others but their own biggest hit—and a defining song of the disco years—was "T.S.O.P. (The Sound of Philadelphia)" (*TSOP [The Sound of Philadelphia]*, Philadelphia, 1973). The song was used for years as the theme song of the TV show *Soul Train*. Another early and memorable M.F.S.B. disco tune was "Love Is the Message" (*Love Is the Message*, Philadelphia LP, 1973). Their song "K-Jee" was on the soundtrack of *Saturday Night Fever*.

STEPHANIE MILLS

At the tender age of fifteen, Mills starred as Dorothy in the Broadway show *The Wiz*. She scored her biggest successes in the disco era with "Whatcha Gonna Do with My Lovin' " (1979) and her 1980 song "Never Knew Love Like This Before" (*Sweet Sensation*, 20th Century). Off the same album, "Sweet Sensation" gave the dance world another jumping tune, though it only reached number fifty-two on the charts. Mills had three more R & B number-one singles: "I Feel Good All Over" and "If I Were Your Woman," from her ninth album, *If I Were Your Woman* (MCA, 1987), and "Something in the Way You Make Me Feel," from her tenth album, *Home* (MCA, 1989).

MELBA MOORE

New York–born but New Jersey–reared Moore started in show business in 1969, drawing attention in *Hair* (Donna Summer replaced her in a traveling production of the musical in Germany). She won a Tony Award in 1970 for best actress for her performance in the musical *Purlie*. Although she recorded three albums during the early 1970s, they didn't cause the sensation that lay in store for her when she paired up with producer Van McCoy for her first big pop and disco hit, "This Is It" (*This Is It*, Buddah, 1975). But it was a Bee Gees song, "You Stepped into My Life" (*Melba*, Epic, 1978) that made her name as a disco artist.

ODYSSEY

Although the song peaked at number twenty-one, "Native New Yorker" (*Odyssey*, RCA, 1977) remains a disco classic. The album was produced by the team that brought the world Dr. Buzzard's Original Savannah Band, with vocals by Lillian Lopez.

THE O'JAYS

The five-member group, originally formed as the Mascots at McKinley High School in Canton, Ohio, changed their name in honor of Cleveland disc jockey Eddie O'Jay, who taught them about the music business. The group found gold their first time out with "Backstabbers" (*Backstabbers,* CBS, 1972), and became Philadelphia International Records' main disco band in the seventies. They were instrumental in shaping the early sound of disco music with "Love Train" (*Love Train,* CBS, 1973), "I Love Music" (*I Love Music,* Philadelphia International, 1976), and "Message in Our Music" (*Message in Our Music,* Philadelphia International, 1976).

P

PEACHES & HERB

The original duo—Francine Hurd ("Peaches") and Herb Feemster—were popular soul artists in the 1960s. After fading out of sight in the early seventies, a new Peaches and the same Herb were produced by Van McCoy. They found new fame in the late seventies with their two big hits "Shake Your Groove Thing" (*Hot!,*

Polydor, 1978) and, from the same album, "Reunited," which reached number one. The "sweethearts of soul" were in the public eye again when "Shake Your Groove Thing" was included in the soundtrack of the movie *Priscilla, Queen of the Desert* in 1996.

BONNIE POINTER

One of the Pointer Sisters, Bonnie left the group for a solo career in the seventies. Her biggest hit was "Heaven Must Have Sent You" (*Bonnie Pointer*, Motown, 1978). Also from this album was "Free Me from My Freedom," popular in the clubs, though it reached only number fifty-eight on the charts.

R

THE RITCHIE FAMILY

Likened by some to a female version of the Village People because of their outrageous costumes, the trio of singers—Cheryl Mason-Jacks, Cassandra Ann Wooten, and Gwendolyn Oliver—was named for their producer and arranger, Ritchie Rome. Rome described the group's first album, *Brazil (Brazil*, 20th Century, 1975), as "soul rhythm, somewhere between the Philly Sound and Barry White." Their second album included their biggest hit, "The Best Disco in Town" (*Arabian Nights*, 1976). This first-ever disco medley sampled "I Love Music," "Fly, Robin, Fly," "Lady Bop," "That's the Way (I Like It)," and "Love to Love You Baby." After the song's inclusion in *Saturday Night Fever* gave them broader exposure, the group traded their headdresses, feathers, furs, and chiffon for red, white, and blue bikinis and leg warmers. The new look and sound gave them their last big hit, "American Generation," in 1979. Their song "Give Me a Break" was included on the soundtrack of the 1980 Village People movie *Can't Stop the Music.*

Vicki Sue Robinson

At age sixteen, the native New Yorker was cast in *Hair,* the first of her Broadway roles. Robinson released her first album in 1976 and was nominated for a Grammy for best female vocalist for the single "Turn the Beat Around" (*Never Gonna Let You Go,* RCA, 1976), the hit song that defined her career. After her big star turn in the seventies, Robinson toured the world, sang radio and TV jingles for such products as Doublemint gum and Downy fabric softener, performed on movie soundtracks, and created a New York cabaret act. On top of all that she continued to be what the Official Vicki Sue Robinson Web site calls an "unstoppable dance icon." Sadly, Vicki Sue died of cancer in April 2000, a month before her forty-fifth birthday.

Rose Royce

They were known as Total Concept Unlimited until Norman Whitfield (of the Undisputed Truth) changed their name to Rose Royce in 1975 and got them a new lead singer, Gwen Dickey. They fronted the soundtrack for the very successful movie *Car Wash.* The soundtrack went platinum, and "Car Wash" (*Car Wash,* MCA, 1976) reached number one. Their second album, *Rose Royce II/In Full Bloom* (Whitfield, 1977), on Whitfield's own label, included full-length versions of "Do Your Dance" and "It Makes You Feel Like Dancin'," as well as "Wishing on a Star" and "Ooh Boy." In 1978, the group's single "Love Don't Live Here Anymore" (*Rose Royce III/Strikes Again!,* Whitfield, 1978) reached number five. The song was later recorded by

Madonna. The group faded as disco faded, though a greatest-hits album reached number one in the U.K. in 1980.

Diana Ross

The legendary Supreme scored her biggest solo hit since her number-one 1970 remake of "Ain't No Mountain High Enough" with her first disco song, "Love Hangover" (*Diana Ross,* Motown, 1976). The song gave Motown its first number-one disco hit. From her 1978 album, *Diana Ross,* came "What You Gave Me" and "Lovin' Livin' and Givin'," which was included on the *Thank God It's Friday* soundtrack. Ross's biggest disco hits were on her 1980 album, *Diana* (Motown), "Upside Down" and "I'm Coming Out." As recently as 1995, Ross remade Gloria Gaynor's classic "I Will Survive" on her *Take Me Higher* album (EMI). Said Ross, "It's very important to bring the good stuff from the sixties and seventies to the new generation."

$\int$

Salsoul Orchestra

Modeled after Philadelphia International's M.F.S.B., the band was organized in 1974 by producer Vincent Montana, Jr., who also wrote and arranged their most popular numbers. A kind of disco big band, the Salsoul Orchestra regularly included as many as fifty members, with large instrument sections such as the eighteen-member violin section. The band was an experiment in fusing funk, Philadelphia soul, and Latin music in a discofied mix. Their first album (*The Salsoul Orchestra,* Salsoul, 1975) includes "Salsoul Hustle," "Chicago Bus Stop (Ooh, I Love

It)," and "You're Just the Right Size," classics of the time. They hit the U.S. again with "Nice 'N Naasty" (*Nice 'N Naasty,* Salsoul, 1976), which peaked at number thirty. Their later albums featured guest vocalists from the Salsoul label, such as Loleatta Holloway on "Run Away" (*Run Away,* Salsoul, 1977) and "Seconds" (*Seconds,* Salsoul, 1982).

SANTA ESMERALDA

Usually described as a "gypsy"-style disco band, their cover of "Don't Let Me Be Misunderstood" *(Don't Let Me Be Misunderstood,* Casablanca, 1977) featured disco vocalist Leroy Gomez. The band also appears on the *Thank God It's Friday* soundtrack with "Sevilla Nights."

SILVER CONVENTION

A German duo known as Silver Bird released the deejay promotional disc "Save Me" on the Magnet label in 1974. An early disco success in the U.K., the track was released commercially as being by Silver Convention. After adding three German women and a string section from the Munich Philharmonic Orchestra, the group hit the top with their U.S. debut, number-one hit "Fly, Robin, Fly" (*Save Me,* Midland International, 1975). One of the first disco songs because of the way it brought the bass line out front, the song won a Grammy for best R & B instrumental performance. Their only other notable song was "Get Up and Boogie (That's Right)" (*Silver Convention,* Midland International, 1976).

SISTER SLEDGE

Kathy, Kim, Joni, and Debbie Sledge had been singing together since their debut in the 1950s at the Second Macedonia Church in Philadelphia. Before the group dropped the second "s" from the first name, Sisters Sledge performed rock and R & B music, had hits in Europe and Japan, and even did a cabaret act that included impersonations of Billie Holiday, Cher, and Dolly Parton. Although they began recording in 1971, they finally broke into the national spotlight when Bernard Edwards and Nile Rodgers, the brains behind the disco giants Chic, "propositioned" them (as Kathy put it) to do something disco. Edwards and Rodgers wrote and produced the sisters' platinum album *We Are Family* (Atlantic, 1979), from which the singles "He's the Greatest Dancer" and "We Are Family" both hit number one in 1979.

AMII STEWART

The Washington, D.C., native hit the top with her number-one Euro-disco hit "Knock on Wood" (*Knock on Wood,* Ariola, 1979). Off the same album, "Light My Fire/1-3-7 Disco Heaven" reached number sixty-nine.

DONNA SUMMER

"The Queen of Disco" won her crown with a string of massive hits. "Love to Love You Baby" (*Love to Love You Baby,* Oasis, 1975) peaked at number two and let the world know that here was a force to be reckoned with. Neil Bogart, head of Casablanca Records, promoted the song by encouraging radio stations to play it at midnight, sponsoring "seventeen minutes of love with Donna Summer." Her next album included the disco cover of Barry Manilow's "Could It Be Magic" (*A Love Trilogy,* Oasis, 1976). Summer followed up with *Four Seasons of Love* (Casablanca, 1976), which included "Last Dance," destined to become a Grammy- and Academy Award–winning Top

10 hit in 1978 after being included in the soundtrack of *Thank God It's Friday*. She reached number six with the gold single "I Feel Love," from *I Remember Yesterday* (Casablanca, 1977). Another 1977 album, the double-LP concept album *Once Upon a Time*, was a sort of mock opera based on the Cinderella story.

Recording for disco giant Casablanca, Summer scored her first U.S. number-one hit in 1978 with another disco cover, this one of Gordon Lightfoot's "MacArthur Park" (*Live and More*, Casablanca, 1978). In 1979, she was at her peak, cranking out hit after hit, including three number-one songs. Off her *Bad Girls* album (Casablanca, 1979), the title cut and "Hot Stuff" both reached number one on the pop charts, while "Dim All the Lights" peaked at number two. Summer was at it again six months later with another number-one pop hit, a duet with Barbra Streisand, "No More Tears (Enough Is Enough)" (*On the Radio—Greatest Hits—Volumes I & II*, Casablanca, 1979). The album's title cut "On the Radio" peaked at number five. In 1980, Summer left Casablanca to become the first artist signed to David Geffen's new record company. Her first album for Geffen, *The Wanderer*, was produced by Moroder and Bellotte, and went gold. Around that time, Summer became a born-again Christian and turned her focus to the gospel music she had loved since childhood.

Summer continued releasing collections of her hits throughout the eighties. In 1983, "He's a Rebel," from the album *She Works Hard for the Money* (Polygram, 1983), won her another Grammy—for best inspirational performance. In 1989, "This Time I Know It's for Real" (*Another Place and Time*, Atlantic 1989) gave Summer another big dance hit. After remaking her greatest hits several times over the years, Summer in 1999 released *Live and More: Encore!*

SYLVESTER

San Francisco recording star Sylvester worked with the Cock-
ettes, the Hot Band, and Two Tons O' Fun before going solo. His
first album produced two big disco tracks, "Over and Over"
(written by Ashford and Simpson) and "Down Down Down."
He had a huge international disco hit in 1978 with the anthem
"You Make Me Feel (Mighty Real)" (*Step II*, Fantasy, 1978), followed by "Dance (Disco Heat)." A song from his *Stars* album
(Fantasy, 1979), "I (Who Have Nothing)," peaked at number
forty. "You Make Me Feel (Mighty Real)" was remade by Jimmy
Somerville and hit number one again in a version by Byron
Stingily. Sylvester died from AIDS in 1988.

A TASTE OF HONEY

Originally a trio formed by members of different bands who
met auditioning for Princess Cruises in 1970, A Taste of Honey
was a quartet by 1978, when they became the first black group
to be awarded a Grammy for best new artist of the year. That
year their debut album, *A Taste of Honey*, went gold thanks to
the success of the single "Boogie Oogie Oogie" (Capitol, 1978).

TAVARES

Massachusetts natives Ralph, Antone ("Chubby"), and Victor
Tavares started out with a group called Linda and the Del Rios
(Victor left the group after it recorded its first album), then
became Chubby and the Turnpikes in 1964. Joined by brothers
Feliciano ("Butch"), Arthur ("Pooch"), and Perry Lee ("Tiny")

Tavares, the band changed its name to Tavares in 1971. The soul group began to make disco music in 1975 with "It Only Takes a Minute" (*In the City,* Capitol, 1975), which hit number ten. Their next release, "Heaven Must Be Missing an Angel" (*Sky High!,* Capitol, 1976) went gold and reached number fifteen on the charts. Their version of the Bee Gees' "More Than a Woman" (*Future Bound,* Capitol, 1978) was included on the *Saturday Night Fever* soundtrack.

THE THREE DEGREES

Philadelphia natives Fayette Pinkney, Linda Turner, and Shirley Porter started out with Swan Records in 1965. They were one of the first girl groups to become disco successes. The Philadelphia trio sang backup on M.F.S.B.'s "T.S.O.P. (The Sound of Philadelphia)," but their own biggest hit was "When Will I See You Again" (Philadelphia International, 1974).

THE TRAMMPS

The group was a joint venture of members of two 1960s Philadelphia bands, the Volcanoes and the Exceptions. Leader Earl Young renamed them the Trammps because people kept saying "All you'll ever be is a bunch of tramps" as they hung on street corners, and because he liked Charlie Chaplin, the silent-movie star known as "the little tramp." After earlier stints with the Buddah label, then the Golden Fleece label—moving toward their disco sound—the group switched to Atlantic in 1975. There, they released disco favorites "That's Where the Happy People Go" and "Disco Party" (*Where the Happy People Go,* Atlantic, 1976). Their best-known hit, "Disco Inferno" (*Disco Inferno,* Atlantic, 1977), was featured on the soundtrack of *Saturday Night Fever.*

Two Tons O' Fun

(See also Weather Girls.) Originally backing such singers as Sylvester on the Fantasy label, Izora Armstead, and Martha Wash recorded separately as Two Tons O' Fun. Their first album (*Two Tons of Fun*, Fantasy, 1979) contains several disco classics, "Earth Can Be Just Like Heaven," "One-Sided Love Affair," and "Got the Feeling." After teaming up with Paul Jabara and Bob Esty, the duo changed their name to the Weather Girls.

V

Village People

Brainchild of French producer Jacques Morali and Ritchie Rome (creator of the Ritchie Family), the costumed macho men had big early hits in the gay disco scene with such songs as "San Francisco (You've Got Me)," off their first album (*Village People*, Casablanca, 1977), and "Macho Man" from their second album (*Macho Man*, Casablanca, 1978). Later hits crossed over to the mainstream and gave the campy group worldwide fame. Biggest of all were "Y.M.C.A." (*Cruisin'*, Casablanca, 1978), which peaked at number two, and "In the Navy" (*Go West*, Casablanca, 1979), which hit number three. The title song from *Go West* reached number forty-five. The song was covered by the Pet Shop Boys in the 1990s. Off their *Live and Sleazy* album (Casablanca, 1979), "Ready for the 80s" peaked at number fifty-two. And the group was featured on the soundtrack of the unsuccessful biographical film *Can't Stop the Music* (Casablanca, 1980).

W

ANITA WARD

Like so many of the black artists whose musical careers began in the church, Memphis native Ward sang gospel and classical music in college. But it was her 1979 hit "Ring My Bell" (*Songs of Love*, Juana, 1979) that put Ward at the top of the disco charts.

WEATHER GIRLS

(See also Two Tons O' Fun.) After changing their name to the Weather Girls in 1982, the duo of Martha Wash and Izora Armstead produced an instant and lasting gay dance classic in "It's Raining Men" (*Weather Girls* Columbia, 1982). Written by Bob Esty, of D.C. LaRue, and Paul Jabara, the song continues to be remixed. Martha Wash left the Weather Girls and recorded with a number of groups in the eighties and nineties, including Black Box and C & C Music Factory. Armstead continued the Weather Girls, replacing Wash with Armstead's own oldest daughter, one of her eleven children. In 1993, the new duo recorded the album *Double Tons of Fun*, which included the minor hit "Can U Feel It."

BARRY WHITE

He established his place in the 1960s rhythm and blues and soul scene by putting together the girl group Love Unlimited and later the Love Unlimited Orchestra. His own early 1970s recordings put him on the solo map as a soul-disco artist, and he remained on the charts throughout the decade. His biggest disco hits were his number-one "Can't Get Enough of Your

Love, Babe" (*Can't Get Enough*, 20th Century, 1974) and, off the same album, the number-two "You're the First, the Last, My Everything." After these successes, White's last time in the Top 10 was with "It's Ecstasy When You Lay Down Next to Me" (*Is This Whatcha Wont?*, 20th Century, 1976), which reached number four. It wasn't until 2000 that Barry White received his first two Grammy Awards, winning for male R & B performance and for traditional R & B performance for his 1999 album *Staying Power.*

WILD CHERRY

The story behind the rock group's number-one disco hit is the stuff that disco dreams were made of. Reacting to constraints—in their case, those of their usual rock style—they loosened up, had fun, and scored big. "Play That Funky Music" (*Wild Cherry*, Sweet City, 1976) sold slightly better than Rick Dee's 1976 number-one hit, the parody "Disco Duck."

Z

MICHAEL ZAGER BAND

Originally known as Michael Zager and the Moon Band, with Peabo Bryson, recording on the Bang label, the group's "Let's All Chant" (*Let's All Chant*, Private Stock, 1978) was a huge international disco hit in 1978, especially in Europe.

ABOUT THE AUTHOR

John-Manuel Andriote is the award-winning author of *Victory Deferred* and *The Art of Fine Cigars*. His writing has appeared in the *Washington Post* and *The Advocate* and other periodicals. A graduate of the Northwestern University journalism program, he lives in Washington, D.C.